THE ANIMATED ALPHABET

Hugues Demeude

With 280 illustrations, 195 in colour

Thames and Hudson

Translated from the French *Alphabets animés*
by Ruth Sharman

This edition © 1996 Thames and Hudson Ltd, London

© 1996 L'Aventurine, Paris

British Library Cataloguing-in-Publication Data
A catalogue record for this book is available from the British Library

ISBN 0-500-27908-X

Printed and bound in Italy

CONTENTS

THE MAGIC OF DECORATED LETTERS

From there derives the art so masterly and wise
of picturing the word and speaking to the eyes,
and by means of forms traced with lines of every sort
giving flesh and colour to momentary thought.

The first-century AD Roman poet Lucan is speaking here in his unfinished epic poem *Pharsalia* about the Phoenician origins of alphabetic writing. It is all too easy for us to forget the sheer mystery of these autonomous systems we have invented and coded, transmitted and stylized. We fumble through their letters, gradually assimilating them, and soon the letters become so familiar that they lose their secret resonance. Words are emptied of substance and letters come to seem ordinary through use.

It is those very letters, however, which give expression to our thoughts, making it possible for us to write and others to read them. They condense the whole of human experience, as that great lover of language the poet Victor Hugo reminds us: 'Human society, the world, the whole of man is in the alphabet. The art of the mason, the astronomer, the philosopher, every science, has in the alphabet a point of departure that is real, albeit imperceptible. ... The alphabet is a source.'

It is a source and a mystery that have inspired numerous artists, beginning with calligraphers, painters and engravers – artists principally interested in the shapes of letters, their pictorial and sculptural qualities. To quote Hugo again: 'The demotic language is derived entirely from the hieratic. Every character is rooted, of necessity, in hieroglyphs. All letters were once signs and all signs were once pictures.' Before it assumes the job of conveying meaning and is thereby reduced to a simple everyday sign, a letter acts as an imaginative springboard for limitless dreams and fantasies.

In the course of time, as the texts changed, writing also changed, as we shall see, in accordance with historically determined principles. These developments were accompanied by a continuing artistic preoccupation with letters. Artists decorated them, draped them and painted them. They brought them to life by giving them human flesh and animal bodies. They glorified them by restoring to them all their evocative richness.

These magic letters have an empowering effect on any who come into contact with them: they take us on a journey into the heart of an ingenuous and disinterested world. This is in some respects the world of childhood, where the word has not yet achieved ascendancy over the letter, and where the letter is an invitation to dream, a promise of strange new visions.

THE ART OF WRITING

Alphabetic writing, which originated with the Phoenicians, passed to the Romans via the Greeks and the Etruscans and was assimilated and transformed during the classical period. Our evidence for this is largely based on scrolls of papyrus, a writing material made from plants that grow on the banks of the Nile – succeeded much later by paper (to which it gave its name). Scrolls dating from this time bear Roman inscriptions written in ink and using upper-case letters. Lower-case letters did not yet exist, although the Roman capital letters varied in size, some being larger and more striking than others. The Roman capitals – etymologically the word 'capital' referred to the head of a chapter – were orderly, angular and solidly constructed. At the beginning of the Christian era this classical Roman script was supplemented by two new types of script, the cursive and the uncial. They introduced a lighter, more supple style of writing, creating the impression of the pen 'running', or 'coursing', across the parchment (hence the name cursive), although the uncial was less fluid and free than the common Roman script and correspondingly less popular. Even if what we normally describe as 'Roman capitals' are not directly derived from this alphabet, the lower-case Roman script served as a powerful leavening agent in the development of our civilization – an influence that we are able to trace through the invention of the book as a system for organizing and displaying texts.

With the dawning of the Middle Ages, the papyrus was replaced by the manuscript. This new type of book was made from cured animal hides; it was durable, easy to handle and could hold a large number of pages. Following the barbarian invasions – during which the Roman script was adopted but not significantly developed in any way – the religious renaissance that occurred from the 6th century onwards favoured a renewal of interest in the written word. This revival coincided with the efforts of the early missionaries to convert the heathen tribes of northern Europe through the medium of the Bible, in which God revealed Himself through the written word. It was the examples of two great men, however, which did most to shape the new monastic ideal. They were Saint Jerome, biblical scholar and Father of the Latin Church, and Saint Benedict, founder of the order which prescribed that every monastery should own a library. In monasteries and convents of the time the writing rooms (*scriptoria*) were filled with calligraphers (*scriptores*) and the copying and illumination of manuscripts, known as *codices*, continued until the 12th century to be an exclusive function of monastic life. During this period many thousands of splendid manuscripts were painstakingly produced throughout Europe, and monasteries in England and Ireland, Germany, France and Italy sought to outstrip one another in terms of diligence and the sheer inventiveness of their calligraphic and decorative skills, which they were all seeking to perfect. The task of a skilled calligrapher was more than straightforward copying: it involved choosing the best script and the best style of lettering for the book in question and using one's skills as judiciously as possible in order to give visible force to the word of God. Such practices reached their high point at the beginning of the 9th century, during the reign of the Emperor Charlemagne, who fostered a cultural revival commonly referred to as the Carolingian Renaissance. Charlemagne, himself a man of letters, regarded books as treasures to be valued like gold. Under his auspices the production of manuscripts

Rococo letters. 18th century, Germany.

became even more widespread and a new script was developed using letters that were readily legible and less ostentatious. The Carolingian minuscule, a lower-case alphabet employing small rounded letters which were both easy to write and easy on the eye, was inspired by the common Roman script and spread throughout the monasteries and abbeys of Carolingian France. Charlemagne himself set the example by commissioning richly decorated manuscripts of great value from the monasteries at Tours, Rheims, Saint Denis and Saint Médard. The script which we owe to his influence was important in many respects: it left its mark on the Middle Ages, was adopted again by the Renaissance humanists and has come down to us via what we call Roman capital letters but ought more appropriately to describe as 'Carolingian'.

THE REINVENTION OF LETTERS

It was through the religious and classical books and documents tirelessly copied in the monasteries that the Carolingian minuscule was diffused, but this vast and varied production began to slow down in the 12th century, coming to an end in the 13th, when the monasteries finally lost their monopoly on book production. During the 12th century the lay world became infected by the intellectual curiosity and eagerness for book learning that had once been the province of the monasteries. People wanted to read the classics and learn Latin and Greek, and secular centres of learning gradually grew up as forerunners of the first universities, with those of Bologna in the second half of the 12th century and Paris at the beginning of the 13th gaining particular renown. Increased demand led to a flourishing trade in books which saw the emergence of the bookseller and the transformation of calligraphy into a recognized profession. Over the course of the following century these new calligraphers altered the style of manuscripts, transforming the Carolingian minuscule into a tall and angular, dry, rather artificial character. Gothic script, as it was called, developed rapidly throughout the Christian world and left its mark on the final years of the Middle Ages. It was very much a product of its time, coinciding with the building of the great Gothic cathedrals and the emergence of the bourgeoisie.

From the 12th century onwards the Church no longer controlled either styles of architecture or styles of writing. What the emerging bourgeoisie wanted was novelty and a little luxury, and they could rely on their business successes and their newly acquired wealth to supply it. The impact of this on book production was that the more luxurious and sophisticated the script the more sought after became the book. And by a process of mimesis the same use of broken lines and suspended masses that characterized the architectural masterpieces of the age was to be found in the new script.

At its most successful, Gothic script demonstrated an elegance which the Renaissance humanists nevertheless failed to appreciate. They preferred the old Carolingian minuscule which they unearthed from libraries and which, preoccupied as they were with the classical world, they assumed was derived from the ancient Roman alphabet and was as such the reflection of that great classical civilization. It was from 15th-century Florence that the new writing reform spread. Its influence was widely felt both in time and in space, since it was this new script which was eventually to form the basis for movable type.

For Victor Hugo in *Notre Dame de Paris*, 'the invention of printing is the greatest event in history. It is the mother revolution. It is humanity's means of expression totally reinventing itself; it is human thought divesting itself of one form and assuming another; it is the complete and definitive sloughing of that symbolic snake which, since Adam, has represented the intelligence.'

This new means of expression, even if it brings a cycle to a close, would help us to remember and to propagate an illustrious art already very much in evidence in the manuscripts, and one which effectively corresponds to Hugo's symbolic snake: the art of illuminating letters.

THE DECORATED INITIAL

In his 1841 essay on the calligraphy of medieval manuscripts Father Eustache Hyacinthe Langlois quotes an extraordinary dialogue from the fifth volume of the *Thesaurus novus anecdotorum*. The dialogue is between a Cluniac, a member of the important Benedictine abbey of Cluny, and a Cistercian, a representative of the order of monks (a strict offshoot of the Benedictines) founded at Cîteaux at the end of the 11th century. It runs as follows:

The Cluniac: Although we do not work in the garden or the fields, we are nevertheless far from idle: indeed, there are some among us who read, while the others are engaged in manual work.
The Cistercian: I know, however, just how idle that work is.
The Cluniac: What makes you say such a thing?
The Cistercian: The fact that words which contain within them nothing edifying are idle and that your useless works are precisely of that nature. I could say more on the subject. But what use is there in grinding gold? What use is there in amusing oneself by painting large capital letters with that same gold? What is that if not a useless and idle labour?

Western medieval manuscripts are much more than just collections of written pages and the Cistercian's criticism of illuminated initials relates to a practice that was as widespread as it was subtly varied. Such decorated and illuminated manuscripts have something of the quality of precious jewels. There were three main areas of manuscript illumination: the large initial letter at the beginning of a chapter or paragraph; the margins of the page; and the coloured illustration. Our Cistercian contents himself with denouncing the ornamentation of the calligraphic miniature, maintaining that it does nothing to inspire virtue or piety. If the decorated initial arouses the austere monk's indignation, it may be because it signals an irrepressible creative urge, and one that was frequently linked to a mischievous disposition.

The fact is that the initial letter has exercised a strong attraction from the earliest times. The practice of decorating manuscripts with illuminated initials goes back in the West to the beginning of the Middle Ages. In the Byzantine Empire at the same period the iconoclastic movement led in AD 754 to the definition of the Doctrine on Icons (the word means 'image' in Greek), which expresses the iconoclasts' objections to the vanity of iconic representations of Christ. The offending images were destroyed, but their cult was revived a century later. In the East as in the West, in the 7th and the 12th centuries, there were therefore those who regarded illustrations of the holy text as unseemly display. What worried these detractors was not so much the luxury of the decoration and the illustration of 'the good word of Christ' as the difficulty in maintaining a strict control over the cult within the context of monastic life. Alongside the scholars and the diplomats and the soldiers there was another category of monk, the pioneer of Western painting, as the study of the decorated initial demonstrates: the artist-monk.

Opposite: *Drogo Sacramentary*. 9th century, France. In this fine historiated initial C, Christ ascends to Heaven.

ONGE
QS
NT
T

NA
UNI
NITŪ
UMRE

DE
OM
PO
ENS
DS
UT
QUI
HODI
ER
DIE
GE
TU
DEMP

TOREMNOSTRUMADCÆ
LOSASCENDISSECREDI
MUSIPSIQUOQ:MENTEIN
CÆLESTIBUSHABITEMUS;
PEREUNDEDNMNOSTRŪ
IHMXPMFILIUMTUŪ;QUI

In the 11th century copyists established a precise relationship between the body and the margins of their text. Before dipping their goose quill into the ink or their brush into the paint they used a pair of scissors and a set square to compose the area of parchment on which they would be working, calculating and constructing a representational frame for themselves regardless of whether their purpose was to preach or to illumine. The decorated initial was integrated into this frame and illustrates, literally, not only the artist's own vision but the classical vision of the representational space as adopted by the numerous scriptoria.

The first step towards highlighting an initial was to extract it from the body of the text and enlarge it so that it stood out from the other letters. Later modifications and additions metamorphosed the initial into a strange creature quite unlike its original self, one that aroused surprise and an interest that extended from the letter to the accompanying text. The most important manuscripts were religious texts relating to Christian worship: sacramentaries, books setting out the ritual acts directed towards sanctification; evangelaries, collections of Gospel passages to be read during Mass; psalters, devotional or liturgical books containing versions of the Psalms; breviaries, books of prayers to be recited by clerics each morning as part of the divine office; and finally homiliaries, books of instruction relating to the Gospel.

From the 2nd century onwards manuscripts were regarded as reflecting the 'good word' preached by Christ. The Gospels, or Evangels (from the Greek *evangelion* meaning 'good news'), were written out and recopied, and manuscripts served to celebrate the act of worship and meditation. There was no good reason why these books should not be decorated and in the austerity of the monastic setting a subtle and delicate art soon grew up whereby every initial became the object of great dedication and care. The decorated letter called attention to itself and, like the vestments which are the symbolic ornaments worn in celebration of the divine office, served simultaneously as a source of pleasure, an invitation to contemplation and a promise of future happiness – the happiness of discovering and recognizing the truth through revelation.

The copyist had a number of different titles depending on his function. The chrysographer, or 'writer in gold' as he was also known, used gold ink and was distinct from the calligrapher (whose job was to write in an elegant hand) and from the tachygrapher (whose job was to write swiftly). Saint Boniface, known as the Apostle of Germany thanks to the reforms he instituted in the Frankish Church in the first half of the 8th century, sought to ban the use of gold in secular books, maintaining that only the Holy Bible should be written in gold ink on a purple ground. Boniface was alarmed by the idea that some of the secular manuscripts inherited from classical antiquity might be as splendid as their religious counterparts and might prove equally alluring. Since he himself witnessed the great flowering of illuminated manuscripts and decorated initials, he was clearly in a position to judge the suggestive force of the images, motifs and colours which they employed.

Up until the 8th century the ornamental motifs that developed in the countries around the Mediterranean relied above all on zoomorphic forms. Pages were enlivened with illustrations of birds and fish, and calligraphers developed a varied repertoire of specimen initials: letters in the shape of animals, birds, fish, flowers and leaves, and also anthropomorphic forms – letters, that is, in the shape of human figures.

In the 7th century the British Isles developed an idiosyncratic style whereby the initials on a single page linked up with one another, often composing strange monograms. It is also to Insular manuscripts (as those from Britain and Ireland are called) that we owe the first historiated initials, that is initials decorated with scenes involving one or more figures. These intricately worked designs, which often have a narrative or symbolic significance, continue to be integrated into the body of the text.

In his book *The Decorated Letter* J.J.G. Alexander tells us that there are two types of ornamented initial, one which is independent of the other letters and clearly identifiable and was used in the classical periods of the Carolingian Renaissance and the Italian Renaissance, and another which is to a greater or lesser degree altered and fragmented and was typical of the anti-classical tendency of the Middle Ages. The famous *Gellone Sacramentary*, for example, dates from the end of the 8th century and corresponds to the first type of initial, although it does introduce a new element by metamorphosing the historiated initial into the figure of a person. In this sacramentary a cross stands for the initial T and is the first representation of the Crucifixion scene in French art. The variety of ornaments used, the diversity of motifs and forms, and the use of gold and vivid colours such as red, yellow and green all combine to make this a highly important and valuable manuscript. Charlemagne, as we have seen, proved himself to be the patron of book production through his cultural reforms, and under his auspices hundreds of manuscripts were produced, fostering the diffusion of the Carolingian minuscule. There was a particular demand for work from the schools of eastern France (extending into present-day Germany), which found themselves obliged to comply with the exigencies of the reforms. Other schools from opposite poles of France – Corbie and others like it in the north, and those south of the Loire, especially the abbey of Saint Martin at Tours – also enjoyed a reputation as brilliant centres of creation. Two centuries later these two abbeys would be producing masterpieces of Romanesque art. At the beginning of the 9th century the famous *Corbie Psalter* (ill. p. 21) set the tone. It contained numerous initials in the shape of human figures intermingled with ornamental motifs and animals and leaf scroll patterns. Referring to the *Corbie Psalter*, [Robert] Massin wrote in his book *Letter and Image*: 'The illuminator of this Carolingian manuscript has designed ornate initials which are a curious mixture of the classical tradition, of a specifically British ornamental style, and of designs reminiscent of Byzantine, Syrian and Sassanid art.' Although the monastic schools were cut off from the secular world, links between the various abbeys, and in particular the exchange of illuminated manuscripts, facilitated the discovery and development of a repertoire of decorated letters. As a patron of monastic production, Charles the Bald was following in the footsteps of his grandfather Charlemagne, and in the time of Otto the Great, the 10th-century champion of Christianity, the Cluniac reforms led to increased links between monasteries.

Under Charles the Bald the influence of the Insular style, as evidenced in the *Corbie Psalter*, is apparent in numerous manuscripts. The interlaced designs attempting, often with a broad sweep, to find the ideal line and the birds' heads that serve as terminals to the letters constitute an ornamental repertoire which provided an inspiration for the Benedictines on the Continent. The influence was also felt in reverse, since the use of leaf scroll patterns to fill out and transform letters while preserving their original shape, together with the historiated letter with multiple figures, spread to Britain from northern France. The *First Bible of Charles the Bald* (ill. p. 16), which originates from the abbey of Saint Martin at Tours, makes ambitious and splendid use of its initials, which are set apart from the text and take up a large area of the page. A letter D combines the chariots of the Sun and Moon with the signs of the Zodiac; a full and rounded zoomorphic letter B is decorated with strange animals that are very expressively drawn; and an S and a V are also clearly identifiable behind a solid downstroke terminating in animal heads. Another 9th-century work, the *Drogo Sacramentary* (ill. pp. 11, 19, 25), offers a fine example of a composition combining figural representations with leaf scroll patterns to decorate the body of the letter. The thick stem and crossbar of a letter T contain rich compartments at their extremities to receive the figure of Christ, towards whom the hand of God is extended. In a marvellous representation which in some respects prefigures the frescoes of the Sistine Chapel this calligraphic miniature creates an additional spatial area to convey the suggestion of a world beyond our own. Another letter, a C, encloses the image of Christ ascending to Heaven.

Letters such as these, taken from well-known manuscripts, were widely imitated during the 10th, 11th and 12th centuries. The Benedictine Order, which underwent major reforms following a lengthy period of political upheaval, turned its attention towards classical works and the different repertoires of the Carolingian and Anglo-Saxon golden age. Gold lettering continued to be employed up until the 13th century, and the use of distinct historiated initials bringing together a number of human or animal figures and suggesting a narrative scene was commonplace, as were, increasingly, the new forms of this type of initial which bore no reference to the accompanying text. The focus now was on the invention of images that were variations on a series of themes. J.J.G. Alexander recalls that 'the initials have been compared to Romanesque carved stone architectural capitals in which there was the same problem of the pre-ordained form into which scene or ornament had to be fitted. Just as all the capitals in a nave arcade will vary, so will each initial in a book. And just as the shape and supporting function of the capital is respected, so also will be the form and function of the letter.' What particularly distinguished Romanesque art was its exuberance and vigour. While its iconographic themes were predetermined by a relatively strict tradition, they nevertheless gave rise to lively interpretations, even if there was sometimes a want of harmony in the representation. Romanesque art principally treated religious subjects, notably the Annunciation, the Ascension and Pentecost. Subjects could also be edifying (to use the word of the Cistercian monk quoted above), depicting in symbolic terms the struggle between good and evil, vice and virtue. Comic elements also found their way into these works, devotional books included: one might find a naked jongleur wielding bells, or an acrobat, or mysterious, imaginary animals, or monks or lay figures with a physical deformity, engaged perhaps in some act of mischief.

In 1115 Saint Bernard established a monastery at Clairvaux that became a model of reform and contributed considerably to the prestige of the Cistercian Order. He preached a return to strictness and simplicity and was vehemently opposed to the varied and widespread use of the decorated initial. In a famous passage he denounces it in the following terms (as quoted by Langlois): 'What use do they serve, these ridiculous monstrosities, these hideous beauties, these elegant deformities which so astonish us? ... Here you will see several bodies beneath a single head; there, several heads set upon a single body. ... In short, wherever we look, such a great diversity of strange forms confronts our eyes that we become more readily engrossed in divining these inconceivable sculptures than in reading the sacred texts and we spend the entire day contemplating one after another, rather than reflecting on the divine law.' The phenomenon was so widespread that Saint Bernard was forced to take action by banning the practice of decorating initials with bright colours or incorporating figures into the design. The practice of decorating initials did indeed begin to die out in the scriptoria, but not in response to the great Cistercian's prohibitions: in fact, Saint Bernard had largely failed to convert the Cluniacs and the book illustrators to his way of thinking. The decline in monastic production was due rather to the emergence of lay craftsmen who gradually assimilated the monastic repertoire of decorated letter styles, which became the tools of a new and highly popular profession. This phenomenon marked a new stage in the treatment of the decorated letter. Carefully painted scenes, well-proportioned letters suitably highlighted and set off, and the quest for balance and harmony all contributed to a renaissance of the calligraphic miniature.

Above left: *First Bible of Charles the Bald.* 9th century, France. The zoomorphic initial B with expressively drawn animals, dominates the page.

Above right: *First Bible of Charles the Bald.* 9th century, France. Initial D, incorporating the Sun and Moon and the signs of the Zodiac.

Opposite: Saint Augustine, *Quaestiones in Heptateuchon.* Second half of 8th century, France.

IN NOMINE DOMINI INCIPIVNT PRAEFATIOES INTERPRETATIONVM BEATI AGUSTI
Genesim & exodo & leuitico & numero Libri VIII
HI INEPTATICUM

Above: Hrabanus Maurus,
De Laudibus Sanctae Crucis.
11th century.

Opposite: *Drogo Sacramentary.*
9th century, France. Several
letters, including a large
historiated T which includes
the figure of Christ, to whom
the hand of God is extended.

Above: *Psalter of the Abbey of Saint Germain des Prés*. 11th century, France.

Opposite: *Corbie Psalter*. 9th century, France. One of the most celebrated manuscripts produced in this influential abbey.

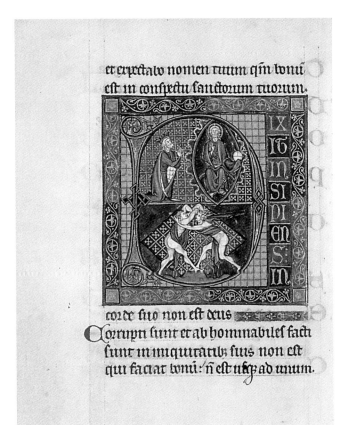

Saint Louis Psalter. c. 1260,
France.

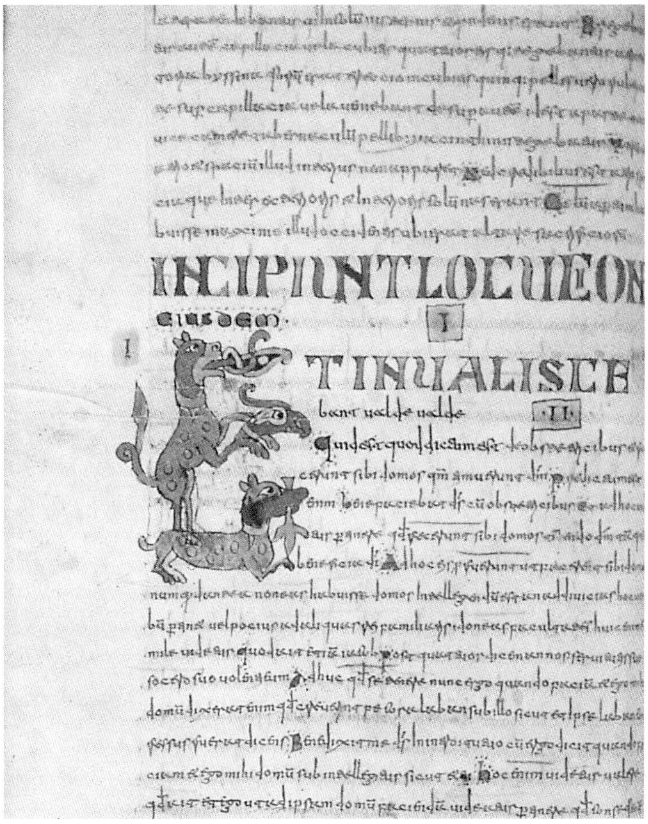

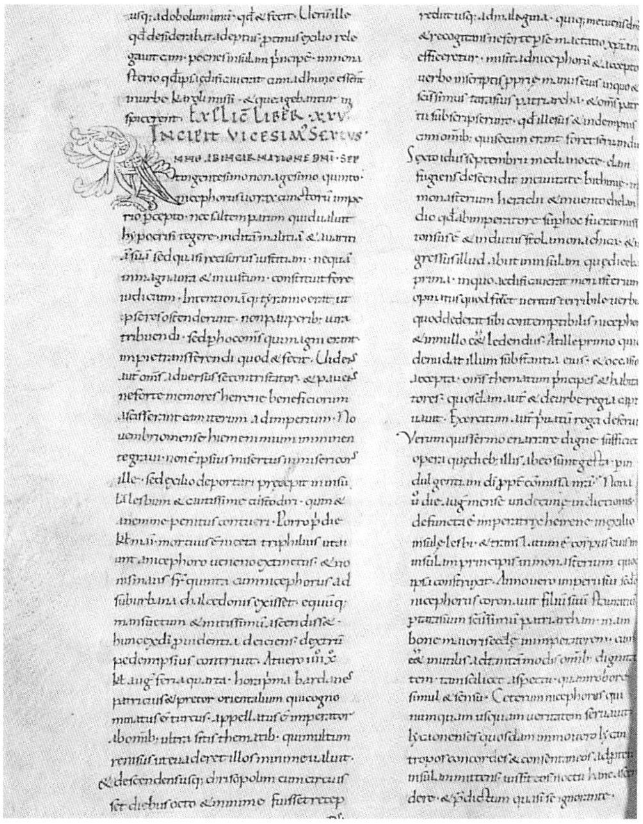

Above left: Saint Augustine, *Quaestiones in Heptateuchon.* Second half of 8th century, France. This letter E is one of the first examples of zoomorphic initials in manuscripts.

Above right: Paul the Deacon, *Historiae Romanae* (additions to Eutropius). 8th century, France.

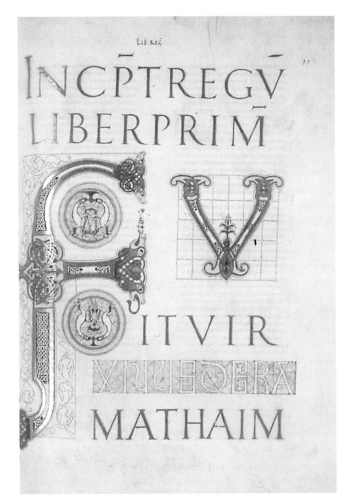

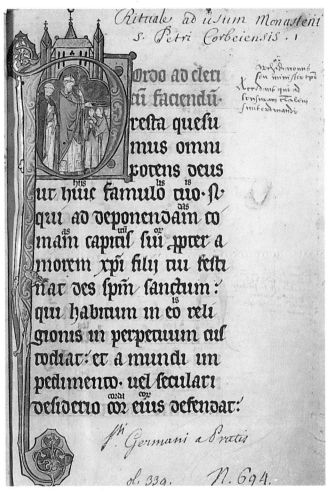

Above left: *Second Bible of Charles the Bald*. 9th century, France. The initial, which is both solid and balanced, terminates in strange animals heads.

Above right: Latin manuscript. 11th century.

Drogo Sacramentary. 9th century, France. In this massive initial D, which stands out from the text and from the page, Christ is nailed to the Cross.

Les Très Riches Heures du Duc de Berry. 1413–16, France.

Les Très Riches Heures du Duc de Berry. 1413–16, France.

THE ALPHABET
ON A HUMAN SCALE

In *Réveils et prodiges* (Awakenings and Wonders) Jurgis Baltrušaitis examines Gothic developments in art and the diffusion of this new style, emphasizing how 'north of the Loire, in an area dominated by the Ile-de-France, profound changes occurred in the plastic arts from the second half of the 12th century onwards. Architecture and sculpture, sculpture and ornament, frame and image were balanced and harmonized in new ways, and both ornament and image came to rely on new principles; but there was neither a sharp break with the past nor a sudden renunciation of all that had been gained over the centuries. The process consisted initially in a revision of values and a shift of emphasis with regard to existing elements.'

It was a little later, in around 1200, that the new Gothic style appeared in manuscript illumination. As Baltrušaitis points out, the new style was marked for some time to come by the fantastic element dear to practitioners of the Romanesque and continued, moreover, to vary from workshop to workshop and from country to country.

Paris was in some ways the nerve centre of the new trend. From the middle of the 13th century its university attracted scholars from all over Europe, and there was a massive new demand for books from the four major fields of learning, as represented by the faculty of the 'arts' (which encompassed grammar, logic, geometry and astronomy) and the faculties of law, medicine and (most highly respected of the four) theology. Booksellers were also in effect publishers and were responsible for the production of numerous books under the direction of the university. Paris at this time was the capital of book illumination, as Dante indicates in the eleventh canto of the *Purgatorio* where he recognizes Oderisi di Gubbio in the circle of the proud: 'Oh,' I said to him, 'are you not Oderisi, the honour of Gubbio and the honour of that art which in Paris is called "illumination"?' Gubbio, who practised book illumination in the second half of the 13th century and worked for the suppliers to the papal palace, shows by his reply just what a distinguished profession this appears to have been: 'Truly I should not have been so courteous while I lived, because of the great desire for excellence whereon my heart was set. ... Your repute is as the hue of grass, which comes and goes, and he discolours it through whom it springs green from the ground.'

It is interesting to note both the celebrity enjoyed by the illuminator at this time and the enthusiasm with which Dante refers to the practice of illumination. With respect, however, to the newly emerging style, it is important to emphasize the distinction that existed between manuscript illustration and ornamentation. There was a shift in illustrative tendencies away from the intense expressivity which characterized the Romanesque and towards a style that embraced strictly human values, notably via the expression of feelings. The ornaments that appeared in the margins of the page, on the other hand, were less reliant on naturalistic forms and demonstrated a marked bias towards the strange and the whimsical.

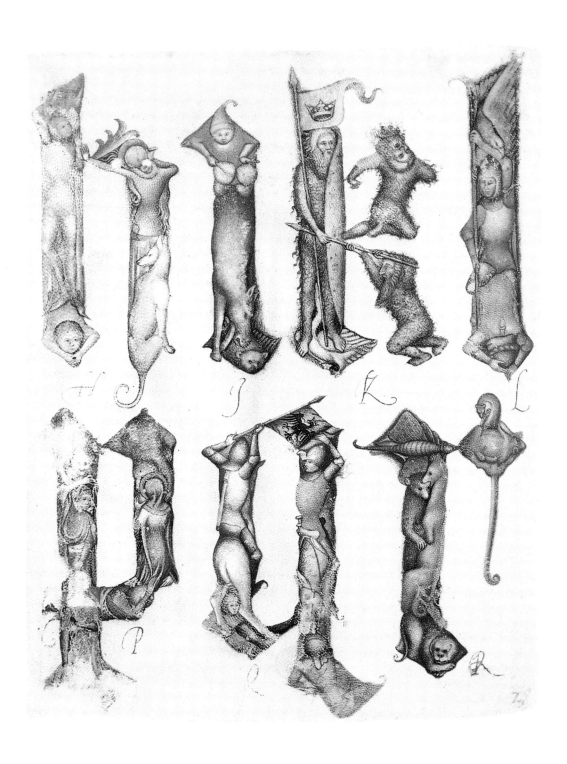

Giovannino dei Grassi,
Bergamo Alphabet. Late
14th century, Italy.

GOTHIC ECCENTRICITIES

Gothic architecture, which had a much lighter, more transparent quality than the Romanesque, created innumerable niches to house human figures and fabulous creatures, and the Gothic manuscript similarly housed numerous strange elements. Unfortunately for Saint Bernard, animals often of a most fanciful kind continued to appear in book ornamentation, demonstrating that this aspect of Romanesque art was still very much alive. Baltrušaitis records the fact himself, citing as examples two psalters famous for their pictorial qualities and representative of the Gothic development in manuscripts: the *Blanche de Castille Psalter*, as it is known (between 1225 and 1250), and the *Saint Louis Psalter* of *c.* 1260 (ill. p. 22). Not only do dragons and large-beaked birds appear within the frame of the miniature, but animals are coiled inside the letters too. In one place a P with its stem prolonged by a type of lizard wraps its loop around a wounded dragon; in another, a broad, tall I serves as the central core of a spiralling tangle of elongated dragons; and a C combines a human figure, a rabbit, a dog and a scroll of luxuriant vegetation. This persistence of zoomorphic designs in the Romanesque style was to undergo distinct modifications, however, in the course of the 13th century. With regard to the letter, animals, and principally dragons, became concentrated within the space of the letter itself and simultaneously intertwined with the leaf scrolls. Romanesque animals were solid, deeply disturbing creatures; Gothic animals were smaller and remained partially concealed by the vegetation festooning the letter. Baltrušaitis calls these animals 'spiral-shaped fauna' and says that by filling the background of the initial they become 'minuscule compositions with the purity and precision of gold filigree'.

The 13th century thus witnessed a renewed interest in the phantasmagorical, although this varied from region to region. In the second half of the 13th and the beginning of the 14th century Paris, for example, seems to have fiercely resisted the depiction of fantastic creatures, particularly in relation to letters – as if Saint Bernard's message had found a receptive audience there. Where ornamentation was concerned, there was a readiness to dispense with such oddities, or else they became secreted within the recesses of the foliage. Leaf designs were greatly preferred to other types of design, and flowers offered the opportunity to copy from life with great precision and to create a representational space that relied on naturalistic principles. There was still some scope, however, for picturesque additions in the shape of dragons' and bird's heads within the body of the letter, but when animals were clearly represented they tended to be drawn from the Carolingian rather than the Romanesque repertoire. In northern France the bias was rather towards Gothic eccentricities. Northern French letters of this time are not zoomorphic, but birds, chimeras and strings of readily identifiable dragons are to be found elsewhere on the page, in particular following the punctuation marks at the end of lines.

England assimilated the new developments in France in ways of its own, developing a more naturalistic approach to leaf designs, but retaining a bestiary of strange and disturbing animals as evidence of the continuing Romanesque influence on English book production. Ornamentation of the ends of lines, originally corresponding no doubt to an overspill from the initial, was also commonly practised in England.

Similar practices are also to be observed in German manuscripts of the time, in which strange figures – which may be clearly identifiable animal forms – are sometimes scattered around the initials. Describing a series of manuscripts from Salzburg dating from between 1240 and 1290, Baltrušaitis tells us that these 'are dominated by splendid initials constructed from Romanesque beasts whose vigour contrasts with the spindly creatures of contemporary Gothic manuscripts. Ferocious monsters come face to face inside a letter A, rise up one behind another in an M, or wrap themselves together and devour the head of a standing figure in the stem of a P.' German manuscripts illustrate the changes wrought by the Gothic treatment of the letter, but also the irrepressible urge to metamorphose it, and German workshops were to exert considerable influence on the development of book illumination.

FIGURE LETTERS AND ALPHABETS

Border ornament and the inclusion of whimsical elements are among the characteristics of this period. Another major feature is the importance of the miniature. Painted on the same page as the text, usually above it, the miniature superseded the initial as the main focus of attention. The miniature came to display increasing precision and its supple, almost three-dimensional, figures helped to create the impression of relief and perspective. By the middle of the 14th century it had assumed the nature of a realist painting portraying an entire world in miniature. Throughout the 13th century and in the early 14th the initial, on the other hand, was most often employed as a 'casket' letter, whose geometric motifs and leaf scroll patterns were carefully arranged like gems in a jewel-case. It seemed, by this stage, to have lost all life of its own.

In France, where this tendency was most widespread, it was not until the second quarter of the 14th century that the historiated initial reappeared in all its glory. The *Hours of Jeanne d'Evreux*, the masterpiece of the celebrated illuminator Jean Pucelle, marked the return of the figure initial, animated once more by living creatures, both animal and human. It was Germany rather than France, however, that was responsible for the spread of this revival.

The end of the 14th century saw the re-emergence of complete figure alphabets. These remarkable pattern books collecting together decorated letters in alphabet form were almost certainly used as models by the growing number of craftsmen. Two that have survived are the *Bergamo Alphabet* (ill. p. 29) and the *Berlin Alphabet* (ill. pp. 42, 43). The second of these seems to stem directly from the Romanesque repertoire and uses Romanesque letters, drawn in ink and embodying human and animal figures. They show young or youngish men, dressed in garments with heavily sculpted folds, fighting with horrible dragons. An extraordinary I depicts a woman languorously draped over a dragon's back; a P represents a young man walking with a basket of leaf scrolls on his shoulders; and the Y shows a dragon wearing a bonnet.

The *Bergamo Alphabet* is even more astonishing. Painted in around 1390 by Giovannino dei Grassi, it moulds a whole host of figures into the form of a Gothic alphabet, superposing a Romanesque bestiary on to carefully executed Gothic letters. The letters have lost their roundness, forming instead precise and complex angles in which to accommodate the figures not of dragons but of men, women, birds, lions, donkeys and much else. They create the strangest compositions. A donkey, for example, standing on a swan faces a man with a lion on his head. One woman has an eagle on her head, another a flying dwarf. Another woman is kneeling down and stroking a dog while behind her a second woman bares her bottom. The M, meanwhile, shows an Annunciation scene. The figures fill up the whole width of the letters, which stand out boldly from the page as a result.

These alphabets were very influential, particularly in the case of the *Bergamo Alphabet*, which appears to have ushered in a whole series of Gothic alphabets, and the decorated Gothic alphabet reappeared in the pages of printed books produced from initials cut on wood. Good examples of these are the Gothic *Alphabet* of Mary of Burgundy (ill. pp. 38, 39) and the alphabet of the Master E.S. (ill. pp. 36, 37), engraved on copper, which uses Gothic minuscules embodying human and animal forms. The Master E.S., also known as the Master of 1466, was without doubt the most important German engraver of the 15th century. His alphabet, which represents a series of warriors engaged in combat with one another or fighting wild beasts, is both surprising and beautiful and his treatment of the Gothic script is as fine as that employed in the *Bergamo Alphabet*. The anthropomorphic alphabet, with its monstrous elements, marked the end of the Middle Ages. When, thanks to Johann Gutenberg, the first printed books began to appear (and by the end of the 15th century almost nine million were in circulation) the need for new complete repertoires of decorated letters and for new and better engraving techniques encouraged artists to push back the boundaries of artistic production. Italy, which witnessed a widespread renaissance of aesthetic aspirations in the 15th century, and which also boasted the best printers in Europe, was to exert an enduring influence on artists throughout the rest of the continent.

THE FLESHING OUT OF LETTERS

The Italian Renaissance adopted a new repertoire of mythological and allegorical themes which accorded great importance to the nude, and artists rediscovered the sculptural beauty of the human body and its harmonious proportions through contact with the world of classical antiquity. This Italian concern with both depth and detail found its way into the history of decorated letters, where it gave rise to a new type of alphabet: the anthropomorphic, or 'human', alphabet whose letters took the form of naked bodies in a variety of exaggerated postures.

The French poet Arthur Rimbaud (who would have seen a few for himself), remarked in *A Season in Hell*: 'I loved absurd paintings, panel friezes, stage settings, clowns' backdrops, signboards, popular coloured prints; old-fashioned literature, church Latin, erotic books without proper spelling, novels of our grandmothers' time, fairy tales, little books for children, old operas, silly refrains, artless rhythms.' When he speaks of 'erotic books' Rimbaud is referring to those bizarre alphabets where the letter is simply a pretext for the depiction of nudity. Customs changed and the atmosphere of unbridled licence that characterized, for example, the French Court under Henri II in the mid-16th century fostered a genre of painting known as '*bergeries*', pastoral scenes spiced with sexy details that even found their way into devotional works. It was at around this time, in 1534, that the first alphabet representing naked men and women appeared. Devised by the German artist Peter Flötner, the alphabet used figures in semi-natural, semi-acrobatic positions without any attempt to disguise their physical attributes (ill. p. 44). The A represents a couple facing one another and embracing; the B shows another couple, this time back to back, in a blatantly sensual position; the M, V and W show women lying on their backs with their legs raised in highly suggestive poses. The letters, which are skilfully cut, are like a series of snapshots that freeze the action of the scene.

Some sixty years later Johann Theodor de Bry, son of the famous Flemish engraver and goldsmith, master of the German Renaissance, Théodore de Bry, designed another human alphabet which clearly displays the influence of Flötner's. The A is once again very suggestive, as is the H, which surely depicts the prelude to an imminent coupling. The naked bodies have been carefully executed and the arrested gestures of the figures are particularly finely observed.

The Italian Giovanni Battista Bracelli produced his version of the human alphabet in 1632. It was to be reproduced virtually without modification two hundred years later by the famous Joseph Balthazar Silvestre, 'the teacher of calligraphy to princes', as he was known (ill. p. 45). Here the eroticism is blatant. Every letter, with the exception of the C, F, I, T and Y, is composed of two or more figures, mostly of both sexes. The A shows a woman sitting astride a crouching man; the E is a woman sitting on a kneeling man's shoulders; the M includes a woman wrapping herself around a man; the U/V shows a female couple.

The Renaissance ended its course by humanizing the elements through which language is expressed – to the great delight of lascivious noblemen.

Florus, *Commentary on the Epistles of Saint Paul.* Initial P. 12th century, France.

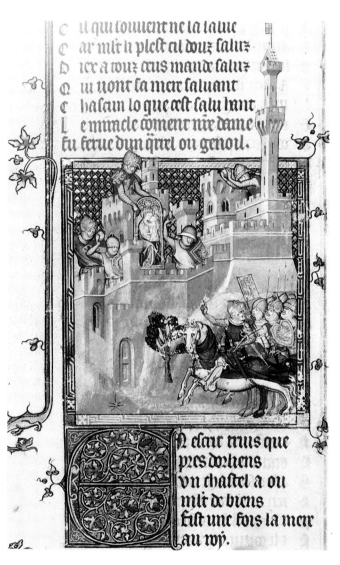

Above left: Jean Pucelle,
Miracles of Notre Dame.
c. 1335, France. The initial
is filled with colourful
dentated foliage.

Above right: Parement Master
(probably Jean d'Orléans),
*Les Très Belles Heures de Notre
Dame du Duc de Berry. c.* 1380,
France. Within the initial,
Herod orders the Massacre of
the Innocents.

Master E.S., *Letters of the
Alphabet*, letters P and Q.
1466–67, South Germany.

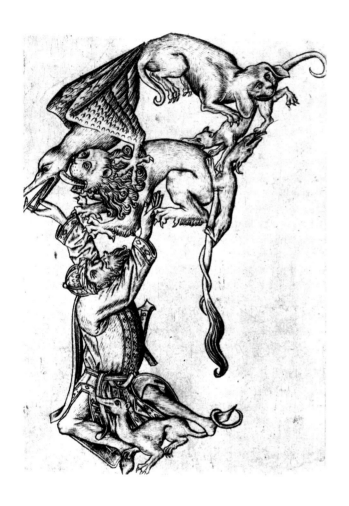

Master E.S., *Letters of the Alphabet*, letters F and T. 1466–67, South Germany.

Gothic *Alphabet* of Mary of
Burgundy. *c.* 1480, France.
The A conceals Adam and Eve
being expelled from Paradise,
while in the elaborate C a man
is being hanged upside down
by the feet.

Gothic *Alphabet* of Mary of
Burgundy, *c.* 1480, France.
The M shows a curious scene
in which a smirking face hides
beneath a grimacing mask.
The magnificent calligraphy of
the T contains a flying Victory.

Above left: historiated initial
A, the Washing of the Feet.
1482, Strasbourg.

Above right: Israhel van
Meckenem, letter D from
an engraved alphabet.
15th century, Germany.

Initials from incunabula.
15th century, Lyons.

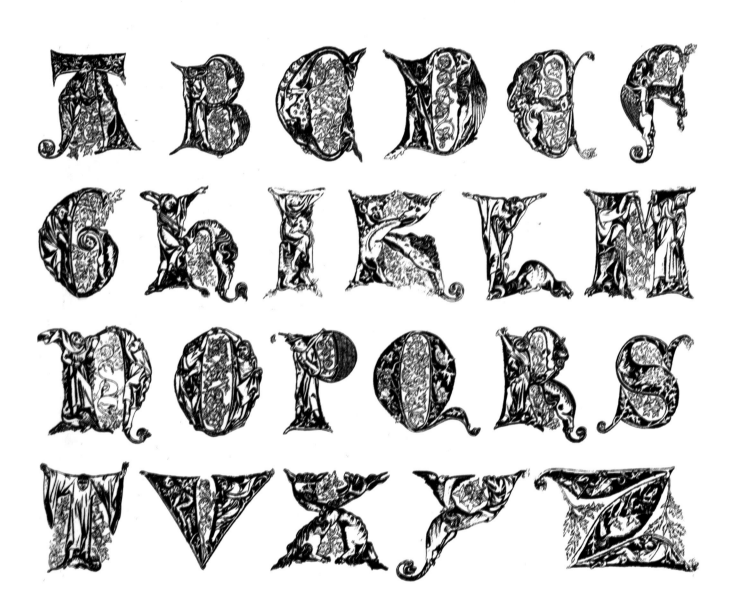

Above and opposite: the *Berlin Alphabet.* Late 14th century, Germany.

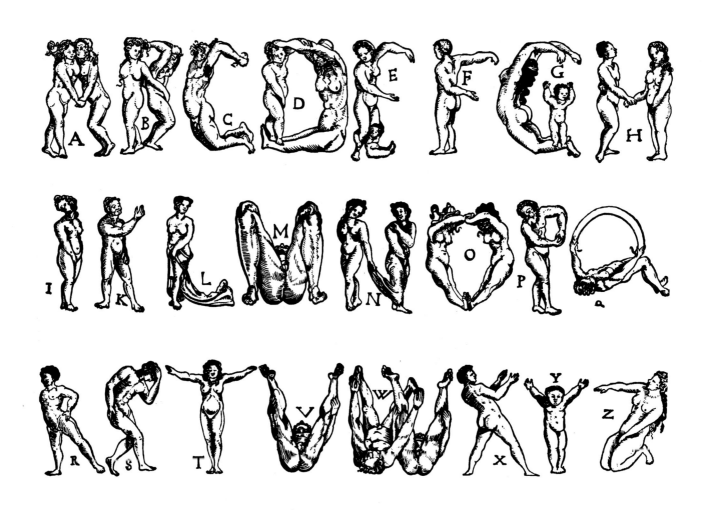

Copy of Peter Flötner's *Human
Alphabet*, engraved by Martin
Weygel. *c.* 1560, Augsburg.

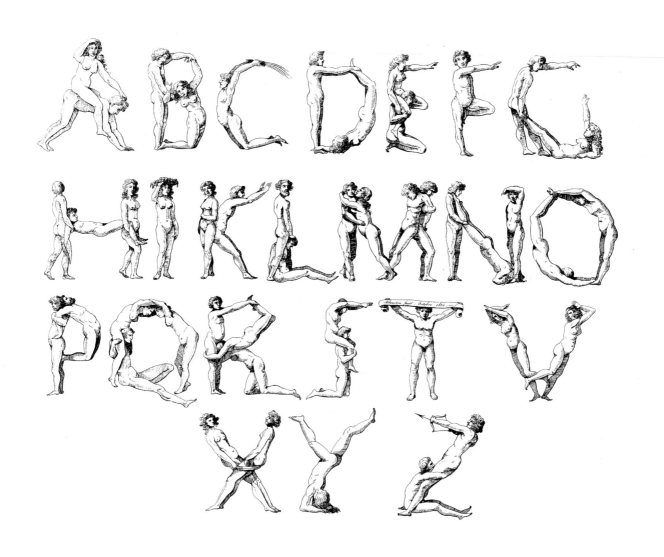

Joseph Balthazar Silvestre,
Human Alphabet. 1834,
France.

THE FRAMED LETTER

Marshall McLuhan, author of *The Gutenberg Galaxy*, a detailed study of the development of typography, describes the transition from manuscript to print in the following terms: 'As the literal or "the letter" later became identified with light *on* rather than light *through* the text, there was also the equivalent stress on "point of view" or the *fixed* position of the reader: "from where I am sitting". Such a visual stress was quite impossible before print stepped up the visual intensity of the written page to the point of entire uniformity and repeatability. This uniformity and repeatability of typography, quite alien to manuscript culture, is the necessary preliminary to unified or pictorial space and "perspective". *Avant-garde* painters like Masaccio in Italy and the Van Eycks in the North began to experiment with pictorial or perspective space early in the fifteenth century. And in 1435, a mere decade before typography, the young Leone Battista Alberti wrote a treatise on painting and perspective which was to be the most influential of the age.' The Renaissance was gathering momentum and was to exert a lasting influence on the art of typography and book illustration.

ARTISTIC TYPOGRAPHY

By the end of the 15th century the spirit of the Renaissance was beginning to make its mark on book production. One of those responsible for introducing the changes was Aldus Manutius, who founded a print works and publishing house in Venice in around 1490 and promoted the spread of roman characters (customarily spelt with a small 'r' in typography). These characters were similar to the script that was in standard usage at the time and inspired the famous French typographer Claude Garamond. Manutius is best known as the originator of italic type, but he is also remembered for his decorative style and his exquisite treatment of initials. In his work the initials are presented within a frame, on a light ground, and are decorated with foliage scrolls and carved leaf designs and sometimes with farandole masks. Manutius paved the way for artistic typography and the Italian influence spread to both France and Germany.

France had a particularly notable typographer in Geoffroy Tory. Born in 1485, Tory became a bookseller in Paris in 1518 and a printer in 1529. He worked for the famous bibliophile Jean Grolier and was himself passionately interested in classical art. Tory's fame rested on a treatise on aesthetics entitled *Champ fleury, ou l'art et la science des vraies proportions des lettres* (Flowered Field, or the Art and Science of the True Proportions of Letters), in which he established a connection between the letters of the alphabet and the proportions of the human body (ill. pp. 50–52). In 1503 and again in 1516 he visited Italy, where he became thoroughly steeped in the spirit of the Renaissance, and through his work on books, perspective and architectural models Tory distinguished himself as the true spiritual successor to Leonardo da Vinci and Albrecht Dürer. He provided detailed commentaries on twenty-three letters and Massin notes that he 'enclosed in the letter O, with its perfect circle, the seven liberal arts, and gave to I ... the task of rep-

Sébastien Leclerc, ornamented
letter. 17th century, France.
Within the frame of the well-
formed and sturdy A is an
intimate scene of Adam and
Eve in the Garden of Eden.

resenting the nine muses. ... Combining the straight line and the circle, these two letters symbolize the two generative organs; from this union, under the sign of the goddess Io, are born all the letters of the alphabet ...'. Tory thus adopts a Rabelaisian approach to the typographical characters that adorn these ravishing works, in which we see him not only dealing with beautiful letters and their importance, but also definitively slanting the art of typography away from the Gothic style.

Tory also responded, in his own amiably mischievous way, to the current fashion for devices and monograms. Discussing a rebus formed by interlacing the letters A and G, he says: 'Jokers and young lovers who play at inventing such things create a felicitous device from the letters G and A; making the A smaller than the G, they place it inside the said G, then tell their mistress that it means: I have a great appetite.' (This is a pun in French, whereby '*G grand A petit*' reads as '*J'ai grand appétit*'.)

THE ORNAMENTAL ENGRAVERS

Albrecht Dürer did much to further the new methods of illuminating the letters of a text as described by McLuhan. The introduction of woodcuts, and in particular engravings of initials, into book production was met in the second half of the 15th century with increasing success thanks to the efforts of printers such as Johann Fust in Mainz and Johann Schoensperger in Augsburg, and many others like them. It was thanks, however, to Dürer that this type of engraving came to assume the same importance as the fresco in Italy. Dürer was the instigator of the German Renaissance and his art expresses a new conception of form based on the discovery of the classical world coupled with strong echoes of his own cultural heritage. The son of a famous goldsmith, Dürer began working on illustrated books in 1493, going on to elaborate four new alphabets (ill. p. 53). In the one book he combined measurements for roman majuscules and the principles for three German alphabets. Dürer's ample, carefully balanced roman majuscules are framed by a dark ground against which little angels are flying, and the liveliness and impression of movement are enhanced by the addition of leaf scrolls. His typographical images reveal what some have called his microscopic vision, and even if Germany remained firmly rooted in the Gothic, Dürer helped to introduce a spirit of reform into the fields of writing styles, printing type and ornamentation.

The famous 16th-century German painter Hans Holbein collaborated with the eminent block cutter Hans Lützelburger and the printer Johann Froben on a remarkable series of decorated initials. Their designs were based on the same principle as Dürer's and used a dark frame to set off roman majuscules, with cherubim cavorting in the background. The letters are suspended within the frame and appear to direct the eye towards the cheery background scenes whose precise, carefully modelled forms have the hallmark of the Renaissance. Holbein also composed a complete *Alphabet of Death* (ill. pp. 54, 55) that was altogether extraordinary in its macabre effect.

During the same period, and still in Germany, Lucas Cranach and Hans Weiditz each produced their own personal version of the alphabet. Weiditz's work is in a similar style to Dürer's and Holbein's, its letters being suspended within a dark frame and decorated with figures of children – up to six within the space of each letter – who play with instruments, leaves or animals. In the work of Cranach (ill. pp. 56, 57), the great painter of the Reformation, the letters are sumptuously metamorphosed into leaves, dragons and cherubs surrounded by fruits and the figures of children and imaginary beasts.

Over the next two hundred years French painters and engravers adopted many of the same techniques for decorating letters, presenting them within a framed space and highlighting them, literally, within a tableau. Claude Mellan and Abraham Bosse, in the 17th century, presented roman typographic letters in the setting of an allegorical painting. In Mellan's work (ill. pp. 72, 73) the letter always presides over the foreground space, physically occupying at least half of it, while appearing more than ever to serve as a key that opens a door on to a world in miniature. In the centre of a meticulously drawn frame an O encloses the eye of the Almighty; an E presents the snake Ouroborus devouring its own tail; a V an ancient suit of armour, and so on. This last image probably represents victory, in fact, so that it is logically associated with the V, just as it is logical for the O to be associated with an eye (*oeil* in French) and the A with an anchor. These charming allegories are the forerunners of the alphabet primers of the 19th century.

At the end of the 17th and beginning of the 18th century French engravers like Sébastien Leclerc, Juan Dolivar and Jean Le Pautre devised similar solutions, though they tended towards greater refinement and a closer alliance with the Louis XIV style. Leclerc, who is famous for his sketches of the Paris suburbs and other drawings from nature, produced full-blown tableaux (ill. pp. 47, 84, 85). The letter, in his work, is as carefully proportioned as ever and the engravings are minutely detailed. The sense of perspective, the exact proportions, the attention to detail and gesture, and the classical beauty of the human bodies turn these miniatures into tiny masterpieces. Dolivar, who slightly predated Leclerc, had set the example by presenting allegorical and mythological scenes or monuments seen in perspective and in relief behind the letters (ill. pp. 82, 83).

One of the effects of the Renaissance on the decorated letter was to illuminate the letter by presenting it in the framework of a pictorial representation, an image. Gradually the letter seemed to merge with the image and to lose its importance, its intrinsic value, but, as McLuhan again emphasizes: 'There is then this great paradox of the Gutenberg era, that its seeming activism is cinematic in the strict movie sense. It is a consistent series of static shots or "fixed points of view" in homogeneous relationship.' It is as if, by placing the typographic letter in the framework of a tableau, artists were endeavouring to evoke its powers of resonance, or in other words its specific capacity to carry meaning.

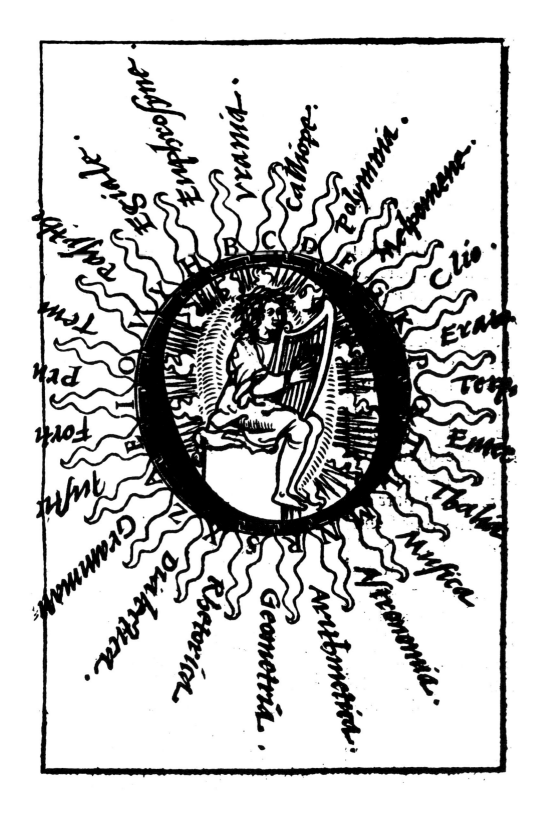

Geoffroy Tory, *Champ fleury, ou l'art et la science des vraies proportions des lettres.* 1529, France. The letter O, representing the sun, is surrounded by the 23 letters of Tory's alphabet and by the nine muses, the seven liberal arts, the four cardinal virtues and the three graces.

b
BACCHVS
CERES ET
VENVS
SONT ICY
MENEZ CA
PTIFZ.

VEla donques comme iay dit, commant le I, eſt le modele & proportion aux lettres At‐ tiques, Ceſt a ſcauoir, a celles qui ont iambes dro‐ ittes. Nous verrons de le O. ou nous ferons le B. qui eſt de le I. & de le O. entendu quil a iambe & panſe qui denote briſeure.

EN ceſt endroit louuant noſtre ſeigneur Dieu, Ie feray fin a noſtre Segond liure, au quel auons ſelon noſtre petit entendement demon‐ ſtre lorigíe des lettres Attiques & auõs voulu ſua‐ der & prier, la quelle choſe encores prions, que quelques bons eſperits ſeuertuaſſent a mettre no‐ ſtre langue francoiſe par reigle, afin quen peuſ‐ ſions vſer honneſtement & ſeurement a coucher par eſcript les bonnes Sciences, quil nous fault mendier des Hebreux, des Grecs, & des Latins, & que ne pouuons auoir ſans grans couſts / fraiz/ & deſpens de temps & dargent.

LA FIN DV SEGOND
LIVRE.

Ordõná ce de le A, faiﬅ de trois I ſus la fleur du Liſﬂâbe.

Notez bien icy, & enten‐ dez.

Geoffroy Tory, *Champ fleury, ou l'art et la science des vraies proportions des lettres.* 1529, France. The A is 'made of three Is', according to Tory, who illustrates it on a flowering iris.

Geoffroy Tory, *Champ fleury,
ou l'art et la science des vraies
proportions des lettres.* 1529,
France. According to Jean-
Henri-Prosper Pouget, 'The Y
was formerly called the letter of
Pythagoras, not because it was
invented by that philosopher,
but because he assigned two
ends to all actions, virtue and
vice, expressed by the two points
of the Y.'

Albrecht Dürer, woodcuts of
framed letters C, D and I.
Early 16th century, Germany.

Above and opposite: Hans
Holbein, *Alphabet of Death*.
16th century, Dresden.

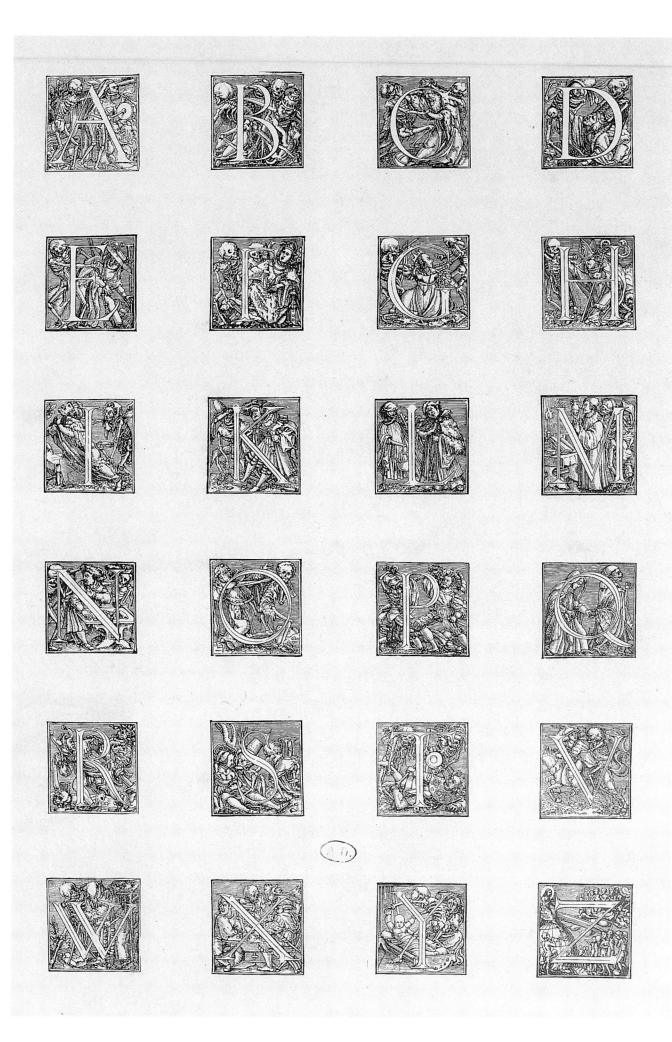

Lucas Cranach, ornamented
letters. 1534, Germany.

Lucas Cranach, ornamented
letters. 1534, Germany.

Above: German woodcuts. Late
15th century, Augsburg. The
letters present biblical episodes.

Opposite: German woodcuts.
15th century. The letters,
standing out from the black
background, enclose scenes of
religious, social and everyday
life, such as the couple in the
U scowling at each other.

German engravings. 16th
century. Gospel scenes with
lavish embellishments.

German engravings.
16th century.

French engravings. 17th century.
Series of Ls for missals.

French engravings. 17th century.
Series of Ls for missals.

Above: Robert Estienne,
typographical characters with
a profusion of detail in their
decoration. First half of 16th
century, France.

Opposite: Engravings by
Langelier, the *Metamophoses*
of Ovid. 1619, Paris.

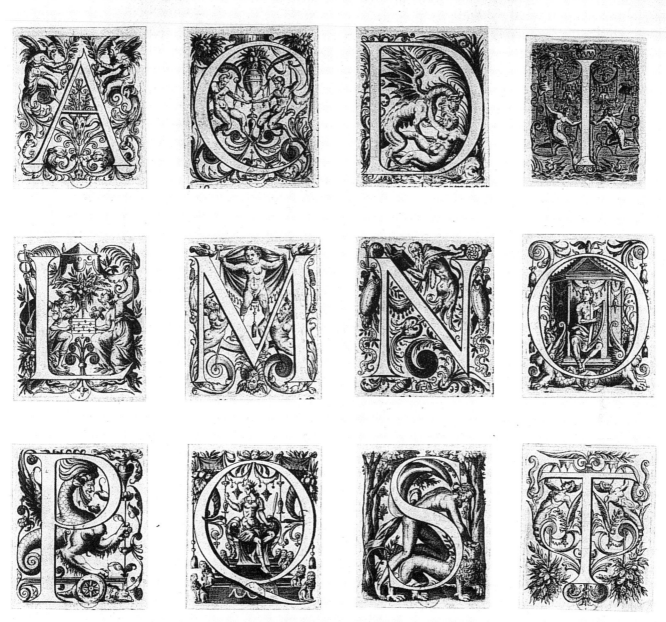

mariage du premier Prince de Rome borna noſtre Diſcours.

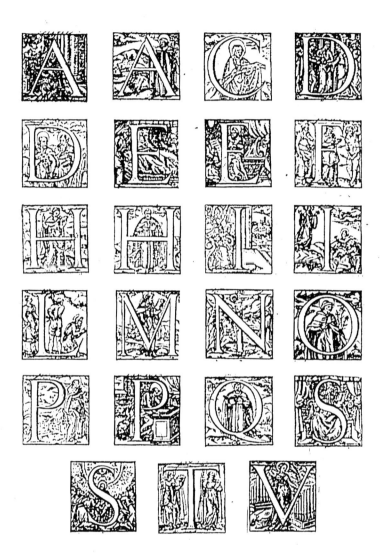

Initials for missals.
17th century, France.

Initial L. 17th century, France

German engravings. 17th century.
Scenes of earthly and celestial life.

French engravings.
18th century. Scenes
of military life.

German engravings.
17th century.

French engravings.
17th century.

Claude Mellan, ornamented
alphabet. Mid-17th century,
France.

Claude Mellan, ornamented
alphabet. Mid-17th century,
France.

Ornamented letters.
17th century, France.

Ornamented letters.
17th century, France.

French engravings.
18th century.

French engravings.
18th century.

French engravings.
18th century.

French engravings.
18th century.

Ornamental letter C.
17th century, France

Ornamental letter D.
17th century, France

Juan Dolivar, ornamented letters.
17th century, France. The letters
are given prominence as part of a
small framed picture.

Juan Dolivar, ornamented letter.
17th century, France. Dolivar's
letters accompany an unusual
variety of themes: here, the
building of the Tower of Babel.

Sébastien Leclerc, ornamented
letter. 17th century, France.
Within a finely drawn and
detailed setting, the L presents
a scene in which a crowned
figure indicates the path to be
followed.

Sébastien Leclerc, ornamented
letters. 17th century, France.
On the right, the S partly
conceals a soldier in a scene
that is filled with lively
movement. Dashing through
the beautifully composed and
balanced S on the left, the
Chariot of the Sun fills the
scene with life.

French engravings. 18th
century. The plain, upright
letters are set into landscapes
that contain a foretaste of
romanticism.

French engraving.
18th century.

THE ILLUSTRATED LETTER

Black A, white E, red I, green U, blue O: vowels all,
I shall relate one day your hidden birth and rise.
A, black hairy corset of iridescent flies
Which, amid putrid stench, horribly buzz and crawl,

Shady gulfs; E, candour of mists and tented skies,
Proud glaciers' spears, white kings, blossoms that, trembling, fall;
I, crimsons, coughed-up blood, the loudly laughing call
Of lovely lips in rage or contrite drunken sighs ...

In his poem *Vowels*, whose first two stanzas are quoted here in the David Ronson trans-
lation, Arthur Rimbaud seeks to convey the intimate associations of those letters – the
jumble of colourful images and layered dreamlike states they evoke for him through
their shapes – and to make visible to us their inner worlds.

Many famous artists, as we have seen, had applied their skills to bringing letters to life
in terms of form, as Rimbaud is doing here poetically with the vowels. Some of these
artists had endeavoured to animate and illustrate entire alphabets by diverting them
from their primary function.

FANTASY ALPHABETS

Some alphabets were drawn, painted or engraved in such strange ways that they give the
impression of having been created in the artist's sleep, as if they belonged to the world
of dreams. These alphabets work on the level of the imagination and their sole purpose
is to carry us off into the realms of poetry and vision.

This is the principle that lies behind the Bolognese artist Giuseppe Maria Mitelli's
Alfabeto in Sogno (Dream Alphabet) of 1683 (ill. pp. 93–95). The first plate shows the
artist himself asleep. The anthropomorphic letters which follow are perfectly executed
and represent beautiful human bodies, many of them virtually naked and drawn with great
accuracy.

In 1570 another Italian, Paulini, had devised a similarly dreamlike alphabet in
which mythological figures, warriors and naked men and women compose the stems
of the decorated initials against a background of historiated tableaux whose subject mat-
ter illustrates the letter (ill. pp. 96, 97). Thus the A shows Actaeon changed by Diana
into a stag; the B Bacchus triumphant; the C Cadmus transformed into a snake, and
so on. The result is a beautiful work, each of whose tableaux suggests a story of its own.

We owe another extraordinary alphabet to the German Lucas Kilian, a famous
17th-century engraver from Augsburg (ill. pp. 102–105). Executed in a baroque style,
this work presents a series of small figures – angels and children – engaged in various
activities within the confines of the richly decorated letters. The world encompassed

Kate Greenaway's Alphabet.
1885, London.

by each initial is whimsical and strange and, despite the excessive flourishes and arabesques, light and full of grace and charm.

In the 19th century the Frenchman Achille Devéria (ill. pp. 114, 115) sought to revive this tradition of graceful and whimsical alphabets which speak as much to the imagination as to the senses. His large initials based on Didot type are at once simple and rigorously constructed. Mingling in their midst are the naked bodies of chimerical creatures, half human, half legendary animal, while the space around them is filled with carefully balanced designs of plants, flowers and fruits. Devéria's alphabet is full of delicacy and charm and captures the spirit of the 19th century – a century which, particularly in France, was to witness the revival of decorated letters and their enrichment through the proliferation of alphabet primers.

ILLUSTRATED ALPHABET PRIMERS

The 'action alphabet', the 'grotesque alphabet', the 'new alphabet', the 'pictorial alphabetic syllabary', the 'illustrated alphabet primer', all became widespread from the end of the 18th century, and publishers of illustrated books now saw it as their job to instruct and entertain at the same time, so extending their range into education. They were helped in this by the development of new printing techniques, such as the invention of wood-engraving (cut on the end grain) by the English artist Thomas Bewick. Using Bewick's method, the block of wood could be cut against the grain, in contrast to the woodcut (made on the plank edge), so removing a number of technical problems and allowing for greater precision in the design. The invention of lithography by the Bavarian Aloys Senefelder in about 1796 gained popularity in France through the work of such craftsmen as Godefroy Engelmann and François-Séraphin Delpech between 1809 and 1816. By using a smooth surface this method of engraving gave greater scope to illustrators eager to experiment with new and complex designs.

Alphabet primers fell into two categories, depending on whether the letter was itself the image or simply the initial of an illustrated word. This latter type of primer was the more common and constituted a kind of dictionary of images, often based on a particular theme, so that animal alphabets and alphabets of the arts and trades (in which, for example, B may be coupled with a baker, C with a cobbler, L with a lamplighter and O with an organ grinder) appeared alongside alphabets of the cries of London (or Paris) or of famous people or military figures. This type of primer – where it was the image (person or thing) which represented the letter – was based on the principle of analogy, aided by the syllabic method. The image evokes the letter, which in turn evokes the syllables, and subsequently the word, to produce a coherent reading.

As interest in the Middle Ages was revived in the 19th century, increasing value was placed on the letter as image, in the tradition of the decorated initial, and it was treated in a variety of different ways.

The letter could be integrated into the design, assuming the form of an object while remaining identifiably itself: a letter A might provide the starting point for a drawing of a house; the bars of a gate might reveal an M, a D suggest a window surround, or an I the pedestal of a statue. For the most part the engraving in these works is very precise, creating a delightful interplay of light and shade. *La morale merveilleuse, contes de tous les pays recueillis et mise en ordre par P. Christian* (The Marvellous Moral, Tales from All Lands Gathered and Arranged by P. Christian), published in 1844, provides a good example of such workmanship.

The letter could also provide the object around which a scene is constructed – a glazier carrying a P on his back, for example, or a sculptor with an L on his head; or a group of figures holding a sheet by its corners and bouncing another L up and down in it for fun; or a woman held prisoner by creepers sprouting from a J (ill. p. 121). This technique of inserting typographical characters in the scene of the drawing was also used in comic syllabary alphabets.

The letter could also simply be placed inside the image, as the framed letter had been. Still in the plain Didot type style so widely used in the 19th century, such letters become part of the representational scene while remaining logically unrelated to it. The foundries which sold letters individually often proposed this type of illustration for use in missals (ill. p. 120), and scenes showing the Last Supper, the Annunciation, baptism and the apostles at prayer were based on this technique. More unusually, the shape of the letter itself could provide the theme of the drawing, representing, for example, a landscape, or a mountain stream, or a tree moving in the wind. Such letters have a light, ethereal quality; typically romantic, they conjure up a whole world of their own.

Nineteenth-century zoomorphic and anthropomorphic letters were a transplant from the Middle Ages which delighted young and old alike. The first of these letters were based on clowns and devils, figures drawn from the collective unconscious, and the first anthropomorphic alphabet (dating from 1826) to combine humour with instruction was entitled *Les Polichinelles utiles ou l'origine des lettres* (Useful Punchinellos or the Origin of Letters). Here we see a series of highly expressive clown puppets contorting themselves into different positions to compose the letters of the alphabet, each letter being formed by a single character, excepting the H, which features two clowns shaking hands (ill. p. 111). The figures in devil alphabets, on the other hand, are like characters in a shadow play, and though hideous and deformed are still able to elicit laughter. An R, for example, represents a lanky body with an elephant head sitting on a grinning demon; an F a cranky professor looking through a telescope at a flying imp (ill. p. 116). A number of engravers became past masters in the art of designing such alphabets, whose attractiveness to children lay in their capacity to amuse and to excite the imagination.

One such engraver was Honoré Daumier, who designed one of the most famous humorous anthropomorphic French alphabets of the 19th century (ill. p. 131). In

Daumier's alphabet the A represents two amiable fellows embracing; the B is a formidable Bluebeard; the D is a dentist examining his patient's mouth; the F is a trumpeter blowing a fanfare; and the V features a terrified man hurtling vertiginously into the void. Another past master of this type of composition was Victor Adam, whose *Abécédaire en énigmes* (*A New Alphabet in Riddles*) of 1833 was published in Paris and also in London and New York. Here each letter is associated with a subject that begins with the letter, but Adam also illustrates the scene with human figures and objects to allow an opportunity for private reverie. Thus, we can see the A as an agricultural labourer leaning on his scythe; the B as a boa constrictor winding itself around a pole; the C as a crescent moon with a human face; the D as two learned doctors in deep discussion, and so on.

In the 1840s Eugène Houx-Marc designed a series of charming action alphabets in which the letters present a variety of characters in different settings. Grandville's *Métamorphoses du jour* (Metamophoses of the Day) of 1828 turns the letters into elephants, mice, dogs and birds that are wearing clothes and portrayed as humans. Jean-Joseph-Guillaume Bourdet's *Alphabet*, which dates from 1836, also manifests a taste for anthropomorphism (ill. p. 130). His N shows a man holding a huge bear on a leash; his U, playing on the story of Jonah, features a young woman in the process of being consumed by a large fish.

These decorated letters were aimed above all at children, who have a greater aptitude than most adults for escaping into a world of fantasy. According to Gilbert Lascault, in a work entitled *Sortilèges des lettres animées* (Sorcery of Animated Letters): 'The letter has not yet been annulled by its absorption into words, which are themselves bound by the sentence. ... Through its shape the decorated letter asserts its materialness before being endowed with any kind of meaning. ... Images and scenes then cluster round, overlay and justify the graphic signifier; its shape becomes the starting point of dreams.'

At this point we may begin to imagine what the poet Rimbaud was seeking to convey through words and what dreams those marvellous alphabets had conjured up for him in his youth.

Opposite: Giuseppe Maria Mitelli, *Alfabeto in Sogno*. 1683, Italy.

G.M.Mitelli F.

A

L'altra lettera pur par che t'esprima
L'affetto ch'a quest'Arte hai da portare
Che del tenor istesso è de la prima

Above and opposite: Giuseppe
Maria Mitelli, *Alfabeto in
Sogno*. 1683, Italy.

G. M. Mitelli Ie F.

D

Del D. non può far il Pittor mai senza,
Se noi uogliam considerar, ch'ei dica,
Neceßaria è al Pittor la Diligenza.

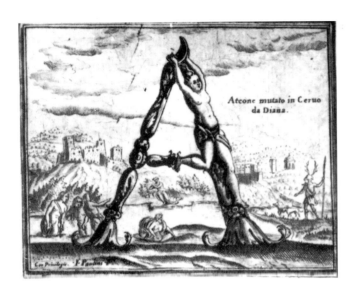

I. Paulini, *Alphabet.* 1570,
Italy. In this extraordinary
alphabet, each strangely
decorated initial stands
within a scene that presents
a mythological historiated
tableau illustrating the letter
concerned.

I. Paulini, *Alphabet.* 1570,
Italy. Above: Cadmus, Aeneas,
Iphigenia and Lycaon;
opposite: Actaeon, Bacchus,
Phaeton and Ganymede, all of
whose names in Italian begin
with the relevant letter.

Above and opposite:
Théodore de Bry, *Alphabet*.
1595, Frankfurt.

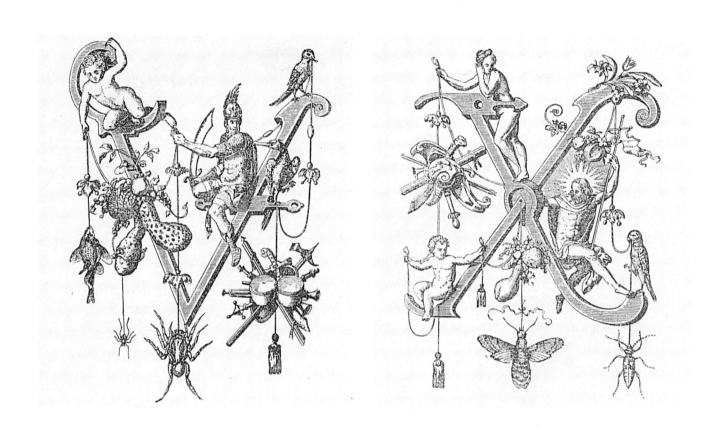

Above and opposite:
Théodore de Bry, *Alphabet*.
1595, Frankfurt.

Lucas Kilian, *Newes ABC
Buechlein.* 1627, Augsburg.

Lucas Kilian, *Newes ABC
Buechlein.* 1627, Augsburg.

Lucas Kilian, *Newes ABC
Buechlein.* 1627, Augsburg.

Lucas Kilian, *Newes ABC
Buechlein.* 1627, Augsburg.

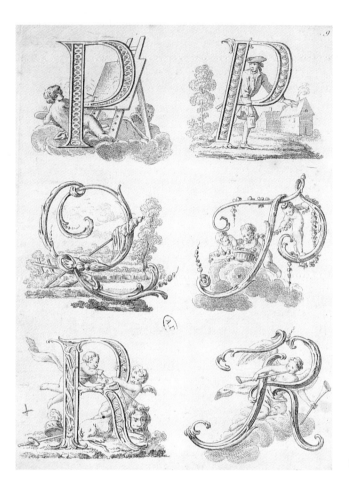

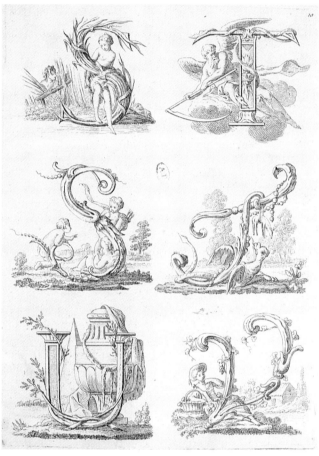

Above and opposite: *Pouget's Alphabet.* Second half of 17th century, France.

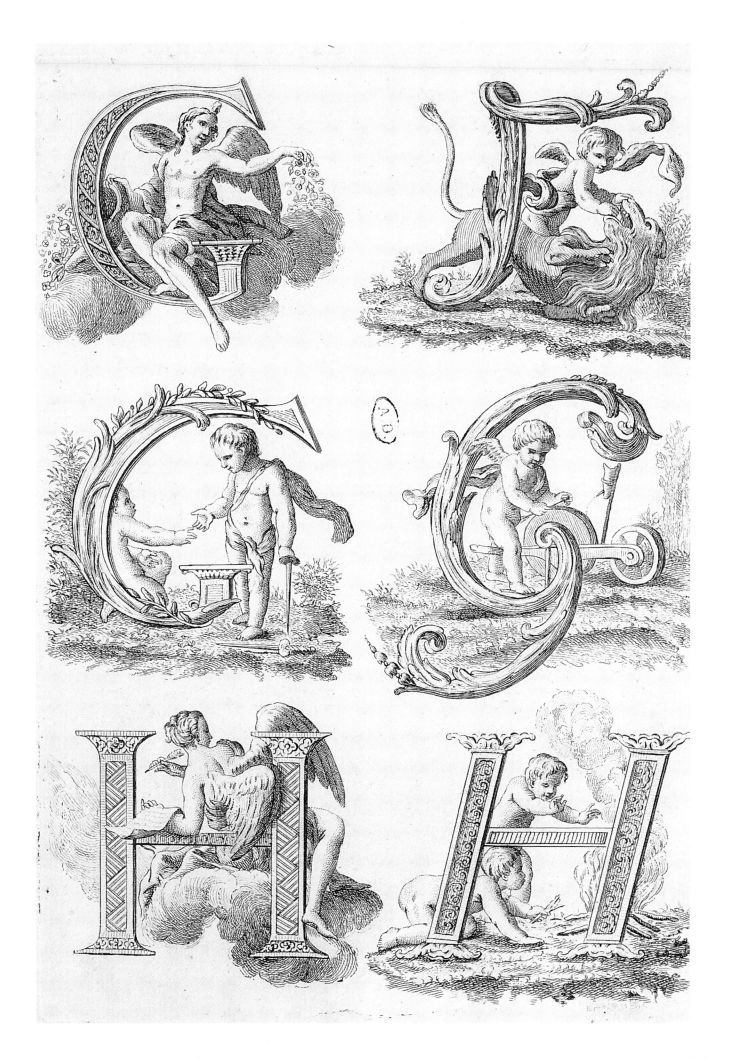

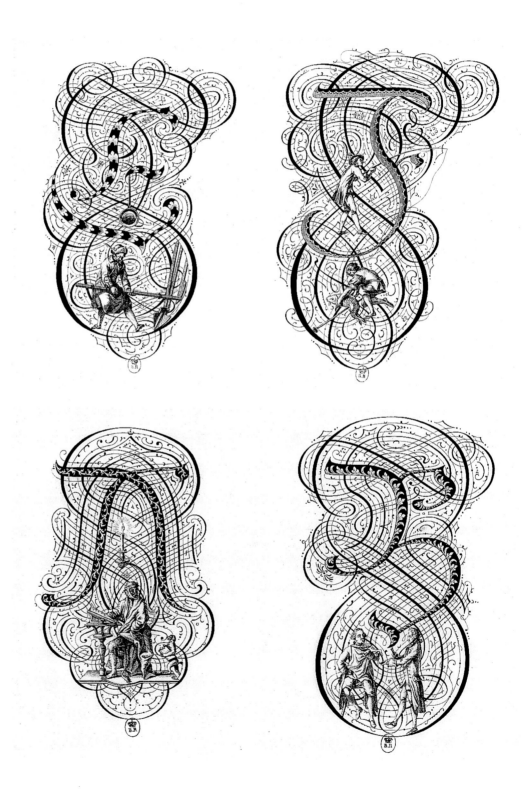

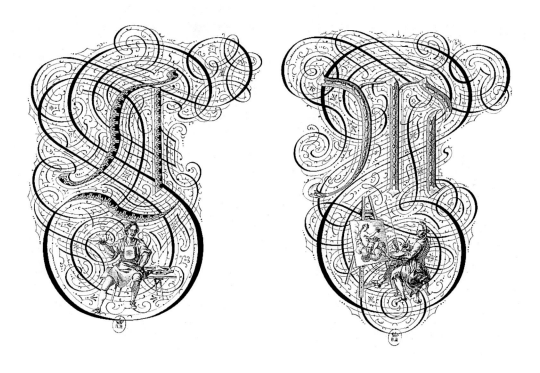

Above and opposite: *Albrecht's Alphabet.* 17th century, Germany.

Rococo letters. 18th century,
Germany.

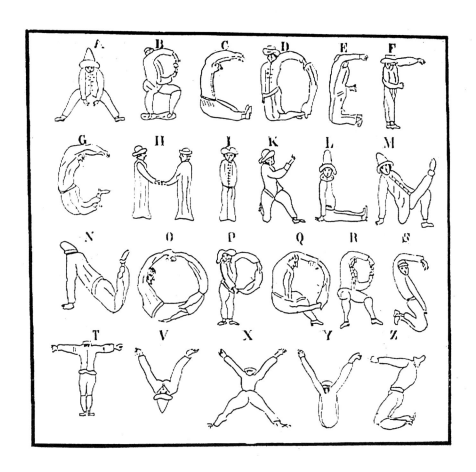

Les Polichinelles utiles ou l'origine des lettres. 1826, France.

Floriated letter, from the first
floral alphabet book, drawn
by Bruchon and engraved by
Colinet. 18th century, Paris.

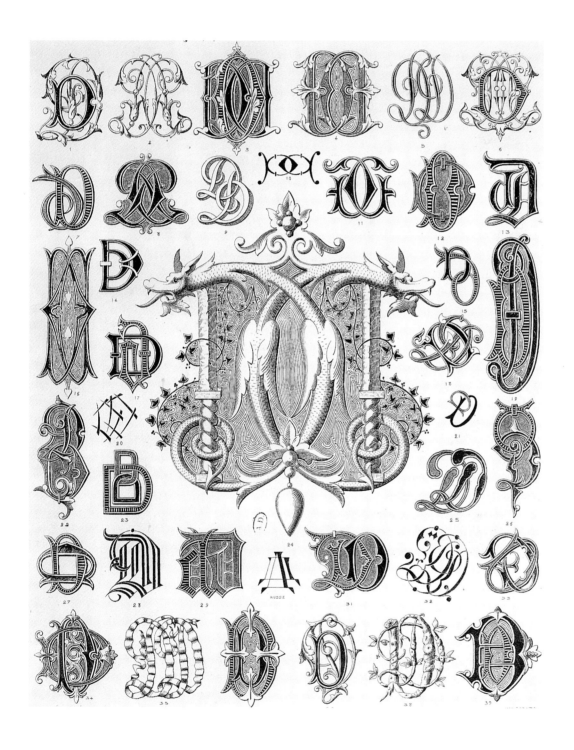

Variations on the letter D,
drawn and engraved by
Leborgne. 19th century, Paris.

Achille Devéria, *Alphabet*.
19th century, France.

Achille Devéria, *Alphabet*.
19th century, France.

Devil Alphabet. 1837, France.

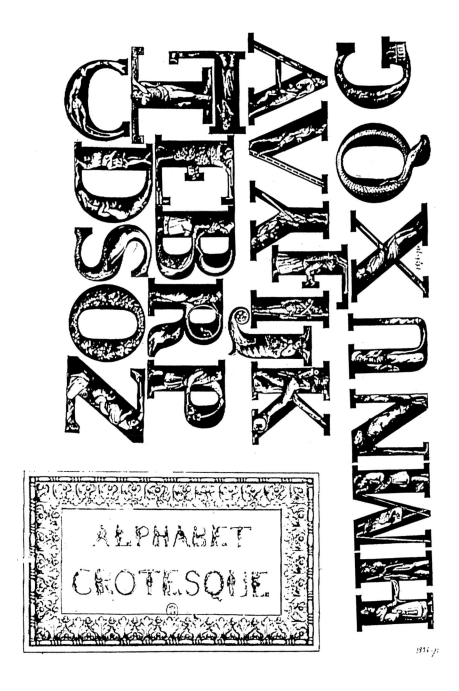

Grotesque Alphabet. 1836, France. The figures are contained within the outline of the typographic characters, renewing in some respect the traditon of 'casket' letters.

New Alphabet. 1838, France.
Each floating letter is a little
self-contained world in which
some event is taking place.

ATTRIBUTS MORTUAIRES

Nᵒ 2843. — 6 fr. Nᵒ 2844. — 6 fr. Nᵒ 2845. — 6 fr.

Nᵒ 404. — 5 fr. Nᵒ 444. — 5 fr.

Passe-Partout. Nᵒ 749. — 6 fr. Nᵒ 2847. — 6 fr.

Nᵒ 2846. — 12 fr.

Nᵒ 2848. — 6 fr. Nᵒ 2849. — 6 fr. Nᵒ 2850. — 6 fr.

Fonderie Générale, rue de Madame, 30, à Paris.

Catalogue of the Fonderie Générale des Caractères Français et Etrangers. *c.* 1850, Paris. New type specimens, even including some alluding to death. Here the M (for *mort* in French) is set in various places of mourning.

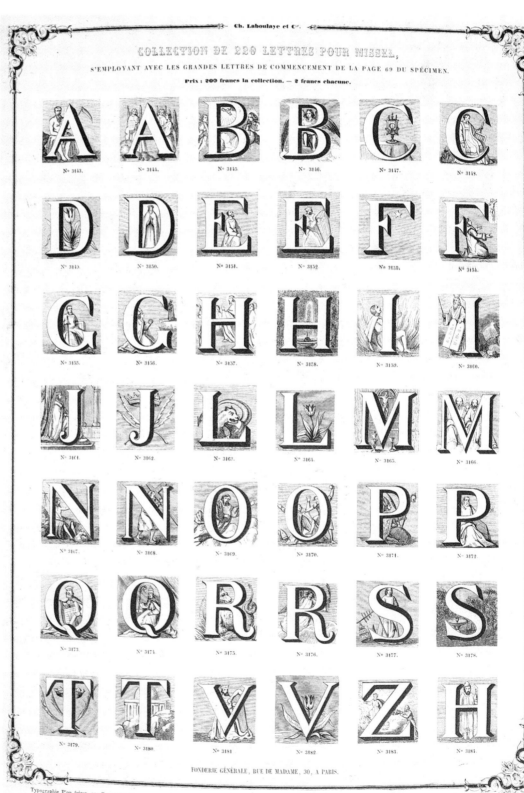

Catalogue of the Fonderie
Générale des Caractères
Français et Etrangers.
c. 1850, Paris. Decorative
initials for missals.

Catalogue of the Fonderie
Générale des Caractères
Français et Etrangers.
c. 1850, Paris.

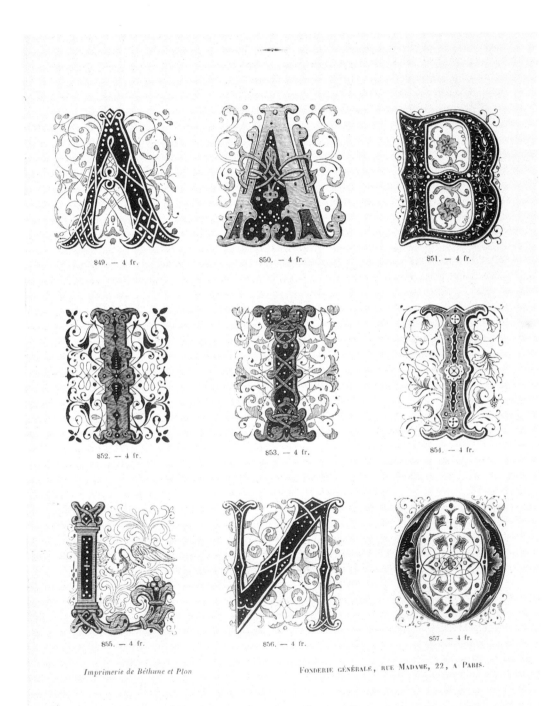

849. — 4 fr.

850. — 4 fr.

851. — 4 fr.

852. — 4 fr.

853. — 4 fr.

854. — 4 fr.

855. — 4 fr.

856. — 4 fr.

857. — 4 fr.

Imprimerie de Béthune et Plon

FONDERIE GÉNÉRALE, RUE MADAME, 22, A PARIS.

Above and opposite:
Catalogue of the Fonderie
Générale des Caractères
Français et Etrangers.
c. 1850, Paris.

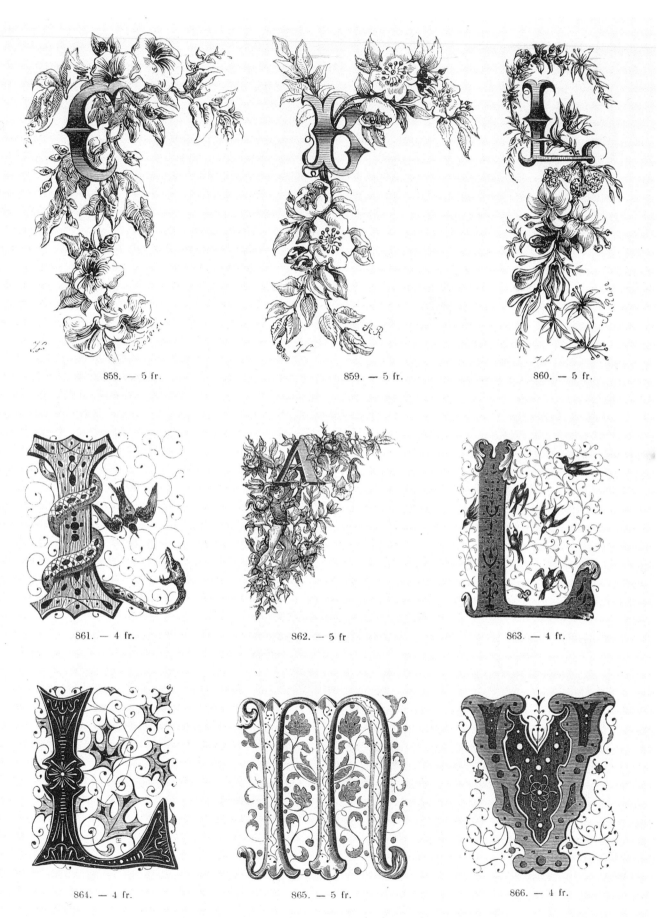

858. — 5 fr.

859. — 5 fr.

860. — 5 fr.

861. — 4 fr.

862. — 5 fr

863. — 4 fr.

864. — 4 fr.

865. — 5 fr.

866. — 4 fr.

Imprimerie de Béthune et Plon.

FONDERIE GÉNÉRALE, RUE MADAME, 22, A PARIS.

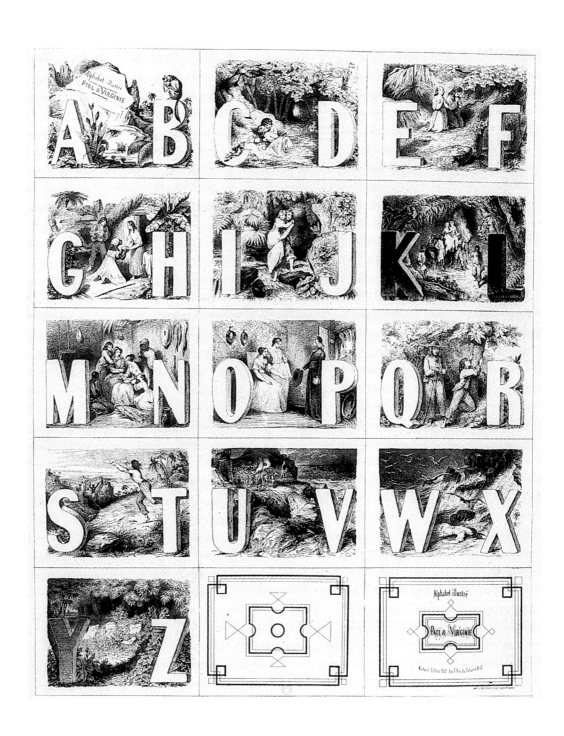

Illustrated Alphabet of 'Paul et Virginie'. 1852, France. The solid, conspicuously placed letters lead one through the sequence of the story.

Illustrated Alphabet of 'Beauty and the Beast' with lithographs by Marchand. 1854, France.

Children's Alphabet, published
by Imprimerie de Lacrampe et
Cie. 1838, Paris.

Children's Alphabet, published
by Imprimerie de Lacrampe et
Cie. 1838, Paris.

Comic Alphabet. 1862, France.

Comic Alphabet. 1862, France.

Above: J.-J.-G. Bourdet,
Alphabet. 1836, France. A
version of the human action
alphabet.

Opposite: Honoré Daumier,
Comic Alphabet. 1836, France.

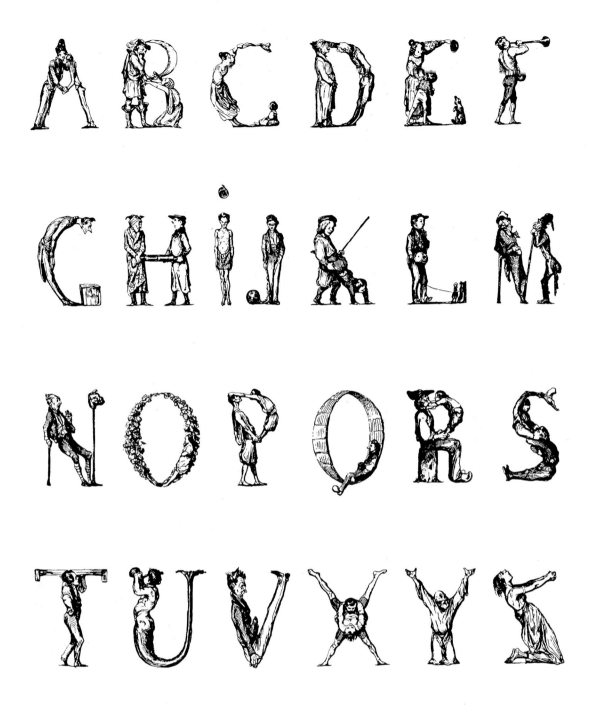

Above and opposite: *Letters for Spelling Books.* Type specimens of the Fonderie Générale des Caractères Français et Etrangers. *c.* 1850, Paris.

Ch. Laboulaye et Cⁱᵉ.

FONDERIE GÉNÉRALE, RUE DE MADAME, 30, A PARIS.

Typographie Henri Plon, rue Garancière, 8, à Paris. (114) A.D. Déposé à la Direction.

133

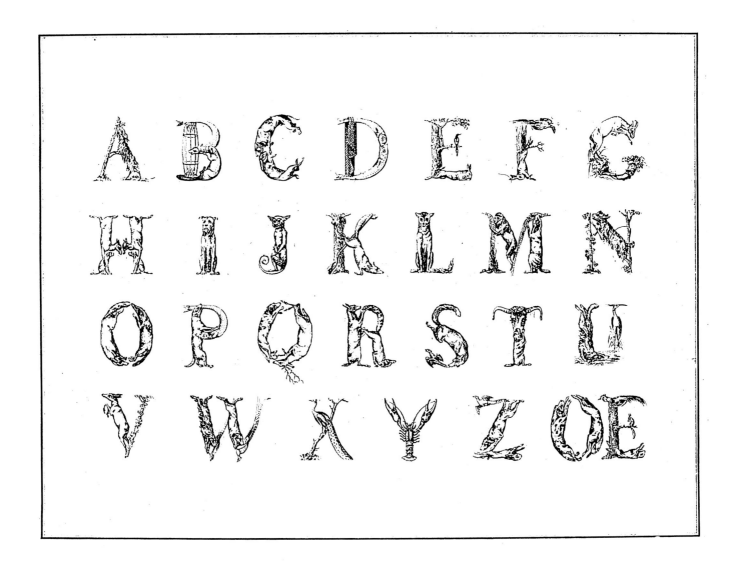

Joseph Balthazar Silvestre,
Animal Alphabet. 1848,
France.

Pictorial Alphabet of the Sea.
1896, France.

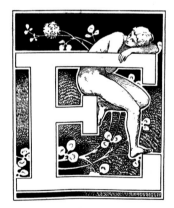

Above: Gerhard Kuehtmann, initials. 19th century, Dresden.

Opposite: alphabet with floral decoration. 1895, Germany.

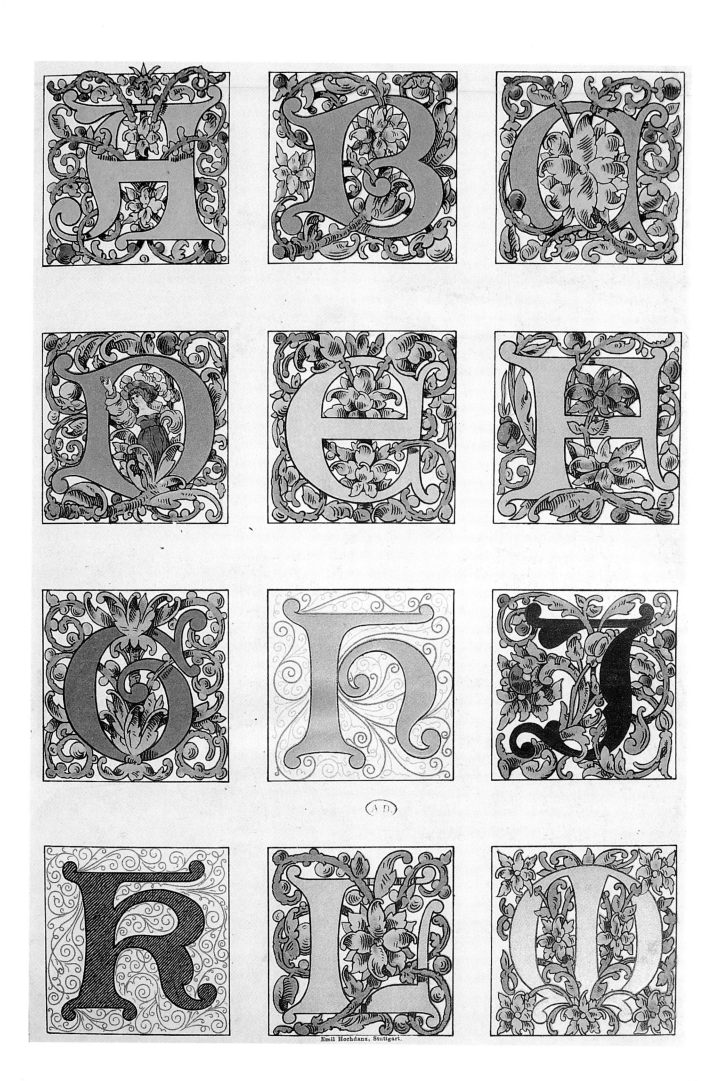

Emil Hochdanz, Stuttgart.

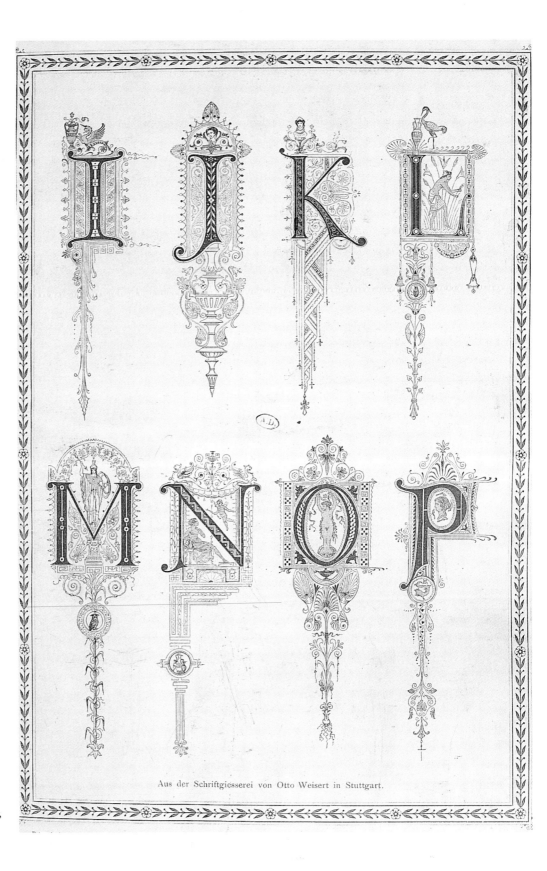

Aus der Schriftgiesserei von Otto Weisert in Stuttgart.

Otto Weisert, initials in antique style. 19th century, Stuttgart.

Competition designs for initial
letters. 1898, England.

Above and opposite: Arcos
and Forain, fancy letters.
19th century, France.

Ornamented letters K and L.
Late 19th century, Germany.

Advertisement for the jewelry maker Janin Closson. Mid-19th century, Paris.

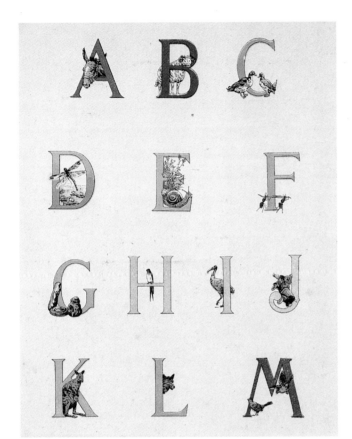

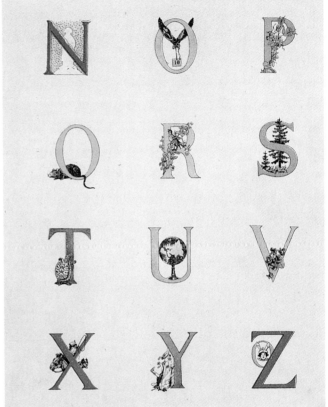

Above: alphabet taken from
the *Petits Contes* of Jules
Lemaître. 1920, Paris.

Opposite: cover of the toy
catalogue of the Maison
du Petit Saint Thomas.
1887, Paris.

Postcards. Universal Postal
Union. Early 20th century.

Postcards. Universal Postal
Union. Early 20th century.

Above and opposite:
postcards. Universal Postal
Union. Early 20th century.

Above and opposite: Paul
Albert Laurens, illustrations
for Pierre Louÿs's *Lêda*.
1898, Paris.

Above and opposite: Miarko,
Animal Alphabet. Early 20th
century, France.

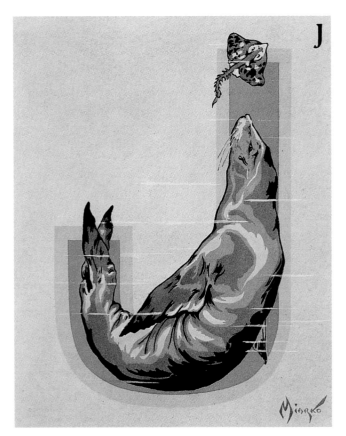

Above and opposite: Miarko,
Animal Alphabet. Early 20th
century, France.

R

MIARKO

Circus Alphabet. Early 20th
century, France.

Circus Alphabet. Early 20th
century, France.

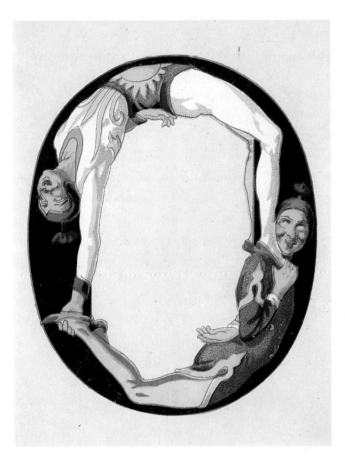
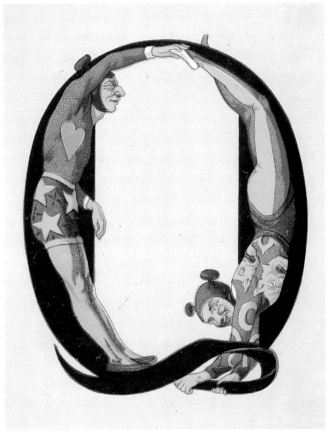

Above and opposite: *Circus Alphabet*. Early 20th century, France.

Alphabet primer.
Chromolithograph. Early
20th century, France.

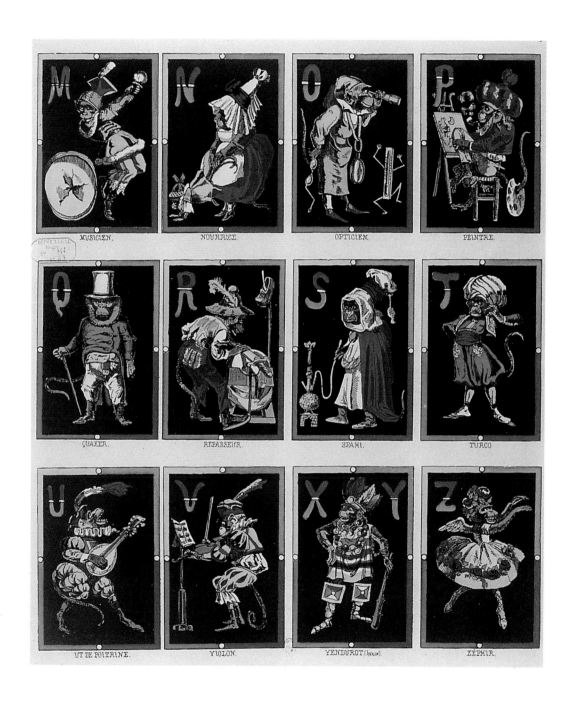

Satirical alphabet primer.
Second half of 19th century,
France.

Above: illustrated letters with
squirrel and magpie. 19th
century, Germany.

Opposite: advertisement for
Bovril. Early 20th century,
England.

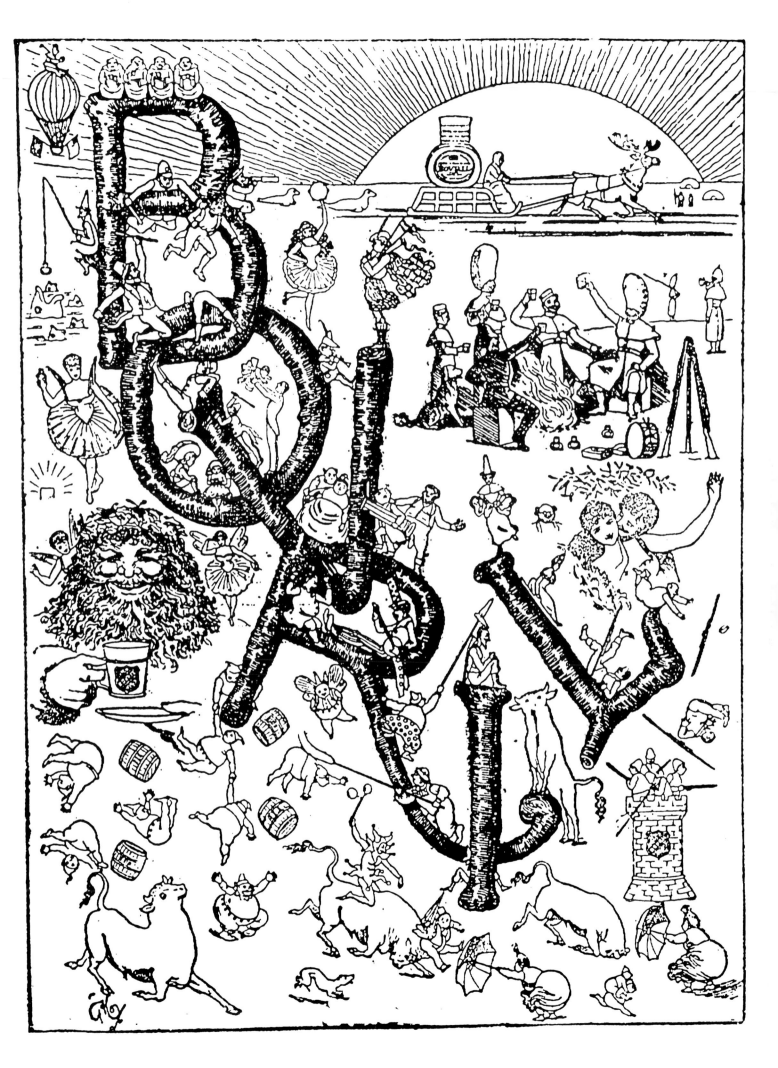

Illustrated letters with
flowers and fruits.
Chromolithographs.
Late 19th century.

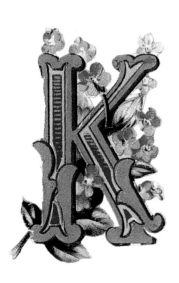

Illustrated letters with
flowers and fruits.
Chromolithographs.
Late 19th century.

THE ACROBATICS OF LETTERS

In *A l'intérieur de la vue* (Inside Sight) the poet Paul Eluard reminds us that 'initials have broad shoulders which provide a definitive orientation for the words that they govern.' Clearly the decorated initial – the initial in its finest form – has broad shoulders, since it simultaneously intervenes, initiates, presents and excites, while suspending the thread of the text. But these specimens that are as strange as they are varied, and as intricate as they are widespread, also have a fine foot and elegant bearing.

One of the settings that perhaps corresponds most closely to the way in which letters have been metamorphosed over the centuries is that of the circus with its acrobats and clowns – the circus as a place for dressing up and disguise, for comic antics and games of the imagination. The first Carolingian manuscripts had their circus element in the guise of acrobats capering among the foliage, and it reappeared in the manuscripts of the late Middle Ages and was present throughout the 19th century. It is the circus which most clearly evokes the quality of reverie inherent in the metamorphosis of letters and which most accurately focuses the playful aspect of these transformations. Ultimately the circus is the world of those who make themselves understood without resorting to words, and by miming the shape of letters calligraphic artists, painters and engravers succeed in conveying the full range of their expressivity.

Opposite: *Allegorical Alphabet.*
First half of 19th century,
France.

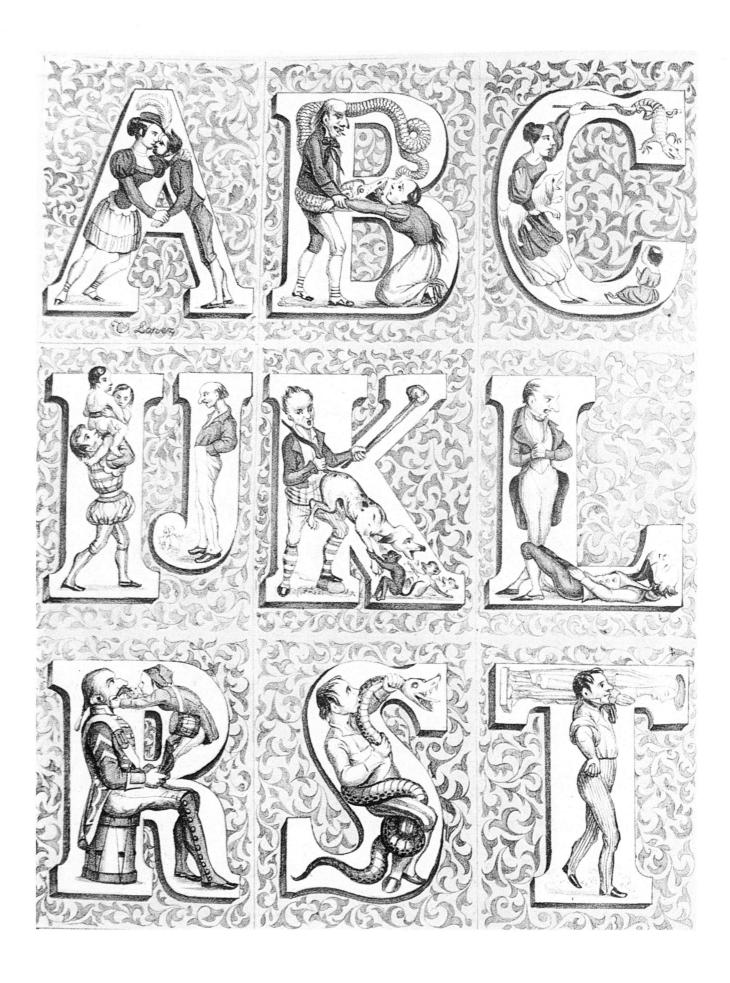

Allegorical Alphabet. First half
of 19th century, France.

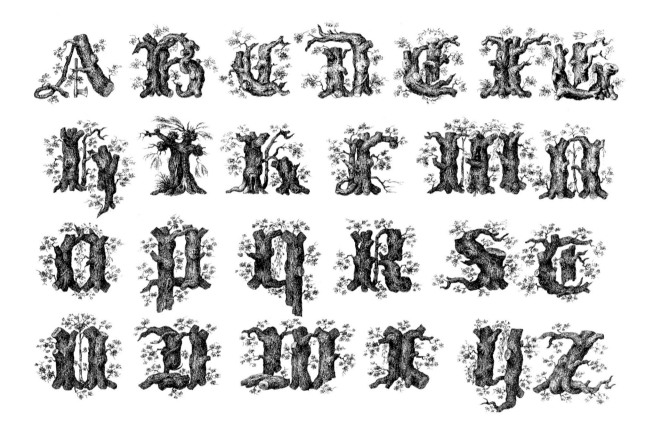

Jean Midolle, *Woodland Alphabet*. Mid-19th century, France.

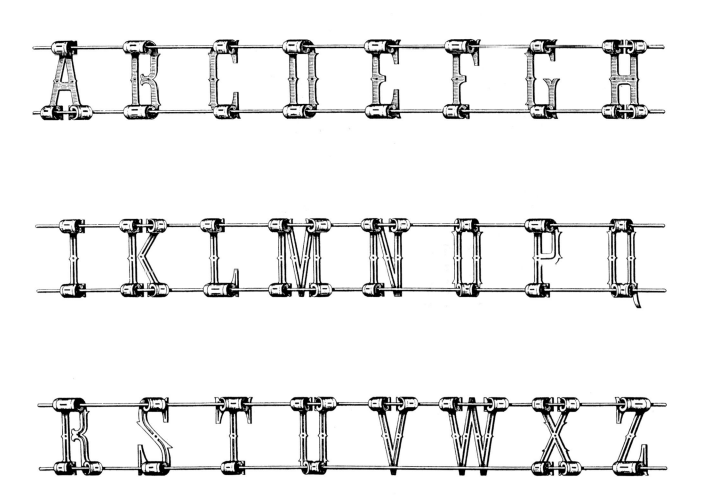

Karl Klimsch, decorative
letters. 19th century,
Germany.

Julius Klinkhardt, *Silhouette Alphabet.* 19th century, Germany.

BIBLIOGRAPHY

Alexander, J.J.G., *The Decorated Letter*, London and New York, 1978

Baltrušaitis, J., *Réveils et prodiges: le gothique fantastique*, Paris, 1960

Bange, E.F., *Peter Flötner*, Leipzig, 1926

Bologna, G., *Illuminated Manuscripts*, London, 1988

Bowler, B.B., *Word as Image*, London, 1970

Calkins, R.G., *Illuminated Books of the Middle Ages*, London, 1983

Clodd, E., *The Story of the Alphabet*, New York, 1900

Dante, *The Divine Comedy* (trans. C. Singleton), Princeton, 1977

Day, L.F., *Alphabets Old and New*, London, 1898

Day, L.F., *Lettering in Ornament*, London, 1902

Debes, D., *Das Figurenalphabet*, Munich, 1968

de Hamel, C., *A History of Illuminated Manuscripts*, London, 1985

Delamotte, F.G., *The Book of Ornamental Alphabets, Ancient and Medieval*, London, 1860

Didot, A.F., *Catalogue illustré des dessins et estampes*, Paris, 1877

Diringer, D., *The Alphabet*, New York, 1948

Dodgson, C., *Catalogue of Early German and Flemish Woodcuts in the British Museum*, London, 1903–11

Drucker, J., *The Alphabetic Labyrinth*, London, 1995

Flötner, P., *Maureskenbuch*, Zurich, 1546

Friedländer, M.J., *Holzschnitte von Hans Weiditz*, Berlin, 1922

Gray, N., *A History of Lettering*, London and Boston, 1986

Gray, N., *Lettering as Drawing*, London, 1971

Gray, N., *Nineteenth Century Ornamented Letters and Title Pages*, London, 1938

Haley, A., *Alphabet: The History, Evolution and Design of the Letters We Use Today*, London, 1995

Harding, A., *Ornamental Alphabets and Initials*, London, 1983

Harthan, J., *Books of Hours and their Owners*, London, 1977

Hugo, V., *Notre Dame de Paris*, Paris, 1831

Jean, G., *Writing: The Story of Alphabets and Scripts*, London and New York, 1992

Johnson, A.F., *Decorative Initial Letters*, London, 1931

Kilian, L., *Newes ABC Buechlein*, Augsburg, 1627

Knappe, K.A., *Dürer: Complete Engravings, Etchings and Woodcuts*, London, 1965

Langlois, E.H., *Essai sur la calligraphie des manuscrits et sur les ornements des premiers Livres d'Heures imprimés*, Rouen, 1841

Lascault, G., *Lettres figurées, alphabet fou*, Lausanne, 1979

Lehmann-Haupt, H., *Initials from French Incunabula*, New York, 1948

Lehmann-Haupt, H., and Petteway, N., 'Human Alphabets' in *Amor Librorum*, Amsterdam, 1958

Le Men, S., *Les Abécédaires français illustrés du XIXe siècle*, Paris, 1984

McLean, R., *Pictorial Alphabets*, London and New York, 1969

McLuhan, M., *The Gutenberg Galaxy*, Toronto and London, 1962

Massey, W., *The Origin and Progress of Letters*, London, 1763

Massin, [R.], *Letter and Image*, London, 1970

Meehan, A., *Celtic Design: Illuminated Letters*, London and New York, 1992

Moé, E.-A., van, *The Decorated Letter*, Paris, 1950

Moorhouse, A.C., *Writing and the Alphabet*, London, 1946

Ogg, O., *The 26 Letters*, New York, 1948

Pollard, A.W., *Some Pictorial and Heraldic Initials*, London, 1897

Reed, T.B., *A History of the Old English Letter Foundries*, London, 1887

Rimbaud, A., *A Season in Hell* (trans. E.R. Peschel), Oxford, 1973

Rimbaud, A., *Voyelles*, Paris, 1883

Roettinger, H., *Peter Flötners Holzschnitte*, Strasbourg, 1916

Rothenstein, J., and Gooding, M. (ed.), *Alphabets and Other Signs*, London, 1993

Shaw, H., *Hand Book of Medieval Alphabets and Devices*, London, 1856

Silvestre, J.B., *Alphabet Album*, Paris, 1843–44

Strange, E.F., *Alphabets*, London, 1895

Taylor, I., *The Alphabet*, London, 1899

Thibaudeau, F., *La Lettre d'imprimerie*, Paris, 1921

Tory, G., *Champ fleury, ou l'art et la science des vraies proportions des lettres*, Paris, 1529

PHOTO CREDITS

Bibliothèque des Arts Décoratifs, Collection Maciet, Paris. Reproductions Jean-Pierre Peersman
Pages: 7, 29, 40, 41, 52, 53, 54, 55, 56, 57, 58, 59, 60, 61, 62, 63, 64, 69, 70, 71, 74, 75, 76, 77, 78, 79, 80, 81, 86, 87, 93, 94, 95, 98, 99, 100, 101, 102, 103, 104, 105, 106, 107, 110, 112, 113, 114, 115, 120, 122, 123, 126, 127, 136, 137, 138, 139, 140, 141, 142, 143, 144, 145, 161, 162, 163, 167, 168.

Bibliothèque Nationale de France, Paris
Pages: 11, 16, 17, 18, 19, 20, 21, 22, 23, 24, 25, 26, 27, 35, 47, 65, 66, 68, 72, 73, 82, 83, 84, 85, 89, 96, 97, 108, 109, 111, 116, 117, 118, 119, 121, 124, 125, 128, 129, 131, 132, 133, 135.

Edimedia
Pages: 150, 151.

Kharbine Tapabor
Pages: 152, 153, 154, 155, 156, 157, 158, 159.

ACKNOWLEDGMENTS

My special thanks to the keepers of the Bibliothèque Nationale de France, as well as to Madame Bonté and the staff of the Bibliothèque des Art Décoratifs.

INDEX OF PEOPLE
AND PLACES

Numerals in *italics* refer to captions to the illustrations.